ABOUT THE AUTHORS:

The material presented in this book comes from the combined knowledge and experience of the authors, Matt Zagula and Attorney Pam Smoljanovich. This brother & sister team is dedicated to helping seniors – and those who love them – to preserve their assets, protect their homes, and secure government benefits to pay for long-term health care.

Matt is a nationally recognized asset protection planner with a practice focused on public benefits and asset preservation for seniors and retirees. His innovative planning strategies have saved his clients millions of dollars over the past 14 years and gained Matt a national reputation as a planning leader with many of America's most respected Elder Law Firms. In addition to helping his own clients, Matt runs an elite coaching group for financial advisors and elder law attorneys. He is a regular featured contributor to *Insurance Newsnet Magazine,* and is the author of *"Spend It Twice, A Retiree's Guide to Free Money."*

Pam Smoljanovich is a practicing elder law, estate planning and real estate attorney in West Virginia, Ohio and Pennsylvania, and a licensed title insurance agent in all three states. Attorney Smoljanovich has been a featured guest on WEIR Radio's Meet the Expert, where she provides valuable information on long-term care and estate planning issues. Pam is a member of the National Academy of Elder Law Attorneys and The Elder Care Alliance. She has a Masters Degree in Rehabilitation Counseling and is a graduate of the Veterans' Benefit Institute. Pam is the co-author of "A Family Guide to Paying for Long-Term Care in These Troubled Economic Times," and her article on costly errors in estate planning documents was recently published in the January 2010 edition of *Insurance Newsnet Magazine.*

INVASION
OF THE
MONEY SNATCHERS

*A Practical Guide to
Protecting Your $tuff from
Creditors, Predators and a
Government Gone Wild*

Matt Zagula
and
Pam Smoljanovich

ISBN: 978-0-615-39503-6

CONTENTS

INTRODUCTION

"Live your life and forget your age"
-Norman Vincent Peale

It has been said that youth is wasted on the young. Of course the old days always look better in the rearview mirror, as our memories become more steeped in happy emotion than hard fact. The feelings of youth are reminiscent of carefree times, when life was simpler, without financial burdens and health concerns. While the older generation shouldered the responsibilities of raising families and "doing without", they also sacrificed their immediate needs to save for the future. But seniors today could not have predicted the uncertainty of the future that has become their reality.

Retirees have lost pensions and health care benefits they were certain would be there after 30 or 40 years of hard work. Seniors are bombarded with warnings about long-term care costs as they watch their friends lose their life savings to the nursing home. Skyrocketing prescription costs force seniors to cut their pills in half or go to Canada in search of cheaper alternatives. Investment and retirement accounts have plummeted, leaving frightened seniors more vulnerable to "get rich quick" schemes and identity theft.

Seniors harbor a very real concern that a decline in health could lead to a loss of independence and autonomy; new retirees fear they will outlive their money or leave their spouse impoverished. And while Government spending is out of control, funds are rarely directed to solving the growing needs of our aging population. Today, more than ever, it's no wonder seniors long for the early days – and the unburdened feelings of their youth.

But what if Norman Vincent Peale is right? What if we could truly live our lives irrespective of age? Is it possible to redesign our lives to recapture some of the contentment and peace of mind we enjoyed in our younger years? Isn't this part of the message of AARP, whose self-proclaimed mission is "dedicated to enhancing the quality of life for all as we age"? Over 40 million members strong, AARP is one of the largest membership organizations in the country. And through its magazines and the radio and television programs it produces, AARP delivers valuable information on health and longevity, nutrition, relationships, employment, finances and other issues affecting those over 50 years old. The predominant message to its members is that life can (and should) be great at any age.

Yet despite being represented by one of the largest lobbying groups in the nation, seniors continue to struggle as they become increasingly vulnerable to health problems with no real financial protection if disability strikes. And while it's no secret that long-term care costs can be financially devastating, or that the death of a spouse can create a huge loss of income, most retirees still fail to plan or take action to avoid what may be the biggest crisis in their lives. This may be due to a lack of awareness of any meaningful solutions, confusion over where to turn for help, or a misguided belief that the government will actually take care of them as they age. Or perhaps it is simply an unwillingness to face what is unpleasant (like the proverbial ostrich with its head in the sand) that causes seniors to ignore the obvious money-snatchers in their future and, therefore, do nothing to protect themselves until it is too late.

The old adage "the best defense is a good offense" has been attributed to the heavyweight prizefighter Jack Dempsey. We have dedicated our careers to empowering seniors with strategies to get on the offensive and wage their own war against a future of impoverishment and uncertainty. Seniors and retirees who have taken charge of their finances and designed a game plan early on, who have tackled and solved financial problems before they happen, are better able to enjoy peace of mind knowing they are prepared for whatever the future holds.

And so it is with that goal in mind that we offer this book to seniors and retirees – a road map to help navigate the rocky terrain of aging in advance, battle ready, so you can truly live your life now and forget your age.

CHAPTER ONE

THE LONG-TERM CARE CRISIS

"If You Know Your Enemy as Yourself
You Can Win a Hundred Battles"
- Sun Tzu, Chinese General/Author

In order to develop an effective game plan for retirement and beyond, it is imperative that we identify those issues that are currently having the greatest financial impact on seniors and retirees. Few would argue that the cost of disability and long-term care is the number one offender. So let's explore what has now become the greatest financial threat to middle-class and upper-middle-class Americans today.

CRISIS IDENTIFICATION

In 2001, the National Endowment for Financial Education sponsored a two-day symposium in Scottsdale, Arizona, to study one of the most critical issues faced by seniors in the

United States. The underlying theme found throughout the report generated from the self-titled "think tank" was that long-term care has become a national crisis.[1] Nine years later, we have overwhelming evidence of a continuing health care crisis as more than 12 million Americans need some form of long-term care.[2] What can be targeted as the cause of this crisis? Well, it's no secret that Americans are living longer than ever before, and as the population ages, we can expect that the need for long-term care will increase proportionately. Since the 1960s, the average life expectancy in the United States has increased almost 20 years. The Baby Boomers are aging – 79 million of them will turn 64 this year. And according to US Census projections, over the next 30 years, the number of people age 65 will increase by 76 percent. This means that by the year 2030, one in five Americans will be a senior citizen! With an aging population facing increased health care needs and rising care costs, and no insurance coverage to pay for it, it is little wonder that we are experiencing a long-term care crisis of such epic proportions.

There wasn't much talk of nursing homes back in the '70s and we never heard of assisted living. But from 1970 to 1990, nursing home expenditures in the United States increased faster than any other health care cost in this country, with a 12.7 percent annual rate of growth. By 1990, 10.2% of Americans age 75 and older lived in nursing homes.[3] Although that number actually decreased to 7.4% by 2006 (due to greater long-term care options for seniors, such as assisted living and home health care) there are still currently more than 1.8 million people living in skilled nursing facilities today.[4] Increased reliance on outside care facilities may be due in part to a shift in family demographics. Looking back to the 1970's in our small hometown, most high school graduates who weren't heading off to college were easily hired at the local steel mill. Elsewhere, they went to work at the local automobile factory or industrial plant – and stayed close to home. Most children didn't have to move far away to find work, and families stayed closer together, in small towns and rural communities all across the country. When an elderly parent or grandparent became ill, it was easier for children and grandchildren to help with care and keep their disabled family member at home.

Well, times have changed. Steel mills closed. Companies downsized. Factories shut down. Not only high school graduates but even adult children have been forced to leave their hometowns to find jobs to support their families or stay employed. And one by one, families have become separated – spread out across the country – and are no longer as easily able to help when dad has a stroke or mom falls and breaks her hip. This shift in the modern-day family is just one of many dynamics that has led us to where we are today: in a long-term care crisis.

Medical advancements and improvements in health care now help us survive things like heart attacks and strokes that were more likely to kill us 40 years ago. Medical technology has produced new drugs, diagnostic equipment and cutting-edge surgeries that add years to the average life expectancy of the American senior. In fact, one study concluded that from 1960 to the year 2000, the average life expectancy increased by 7 years, 3.5 of which can be attributable to improvements in health care.[5] So an advanced health care system is keeping seniors alive well into their 80's and 90's, often well past their initial projected life expectancy.

According to the Bureau of Labor Statistics, a healthy couple in their mid-60s have a 50% chance that one spouse will live beyond his or her 91st birthday.[6] And while that may sound like a good thing, as life expectancies increase, so will the demand for nursing homes. The longer we live, the more susceptible we become to other illnesses that typically affect the aged, such as Alzheimer's disease, vascular dementia, and severe mobility problems. These conditions, like many that affect the elderly, don't respond well to medications and surgeries, and aren't easily or successfully treated or cured. Instead, as these illnesses progress, they often lead to a need for custodial care – and lead the aging senior down the path to the poorhouse trying to pay for that care.

The average cost of a nursing home stay is $75,000 per year! And these costs have been rising at a rate of approximately 6% each year. That is a retirement expense that was never contemplated by most seniors, and their financial portfolios could never take that kind of a hit. Government programs like Medicare and Medicaid were not initially designed to handle the number of seniors who are in need of care today. And as you will see, Medicare turns its back on seniors in their greatest time of need, and doesn't care about long-term care. Without any help from government or private insurance, how long will it take for your money to run out if you get stuck with a monthly bill of $7,000 or more? How many senior citizens could afford that bill? More and more aging seniors, declining health with rising life expectancy, an increased need for health care and no way to pay for it: **Crisis Identified**.

MEDICARE - THE VANISHING GOVERNMENT BENEFIT

Despite the rapidly increasing need for long-term care services, and the rising costs of those services, most seniors and their families are still shocked to learn that Medicare doesn't pay for nursing home or assisted living costs. They mistakenly believe that Medicare is going to take care of them forever, like it has in the past. Unfortunately, this false sense of security contributes to inaction - the failure to plan ahead - which can be financially devastating when disability strikes. The reality is: Medicare doesn't care about long-term care.

Mary Johnson was beside herself. John, her husband of 50 years, had a severe stroke five weeks ago. John had been hospitalized for several weeks; first in acute care and then on a skilled floor for rehabilitation. John's doctor then released him from the hospital and he was transferred to a nursing home for additional therapy. Mary, like so many others, believed that Medicare would cover the cost of his rehabilitation. When someone told her Medicare wouldn't last forever, she still thought it would definitely pay for the first 100 days of therapy. Mary mistakenly assumed that John's "one hundred days" started when he entered the nursing home, but that is not accurate. John's Medicare days started at the hospital when he began receiving rehabilitation on the skilled floor. By the time John went to the nursing home, he had already used some of those Medicare days to pay for the rehabilitation at the hospital. Let's assume that John makes some progress in physical and speech therapy at the nursing home for a few weeks but by the third week his progress slows down and then stops. Mary is worried that her husband has become depressed because he is in the nursing home and may have given up; or perhaps his medication is affecting his ability to do the exercises. She feels helpless and doesn't know what to do to get her husband to keep improving. John's physical therapist reports to his doctor, who reports to Medicare, that John is no longer showing improvement. Then Mary gets a call from the social worker at the nursing home – she has received notice from Medicare, stating that because he is no longer making progress in his therapy, John is no longer considered to be rehabilitating; therefore, Medicare is shutting off and will no longer pay his nursing home bill. But wait: What about his "one hundred days?" Well you don't always get to use those one hundred days, and in John's case Medicare abandoned him much earlier. Mary is distraught. **How can she afford to pay a $7,000 a month nursing home bill? Where will they get the money? What's going to happen to her husband? What's going to happen to her?**

So many people just like Mary and John are abandoned by Medicare in their greatest time of need. Because the maximum amount of time that Medicare will pay for skilled care is 100 days – but the average number of days actually paid for is much less. Provided the patient has spent three days in the hospital first, and is then transferred to the nursing home from the hospital, Medicare will typically pay 100% of the first 20 days of the patient's stay at a Medicare-certified skilled nursing care facility. Afterwards, the patient is responsible for a co-pay of roughly $130.00 per day, and Medicare may pay the balance due to the nursing home for an additional

80 days. However, Medicare's continued payment is contingent on the patient receiving rehabilitation and showing improvement with therapy. If you hit a plateau and stop improving, or your therapist and physician determine that no additional rehabilitation is warranted or possible (like a patient with dementia or Alzheimer's Disease), Medicare will shut off with no warning, leaving you scrambling to find alternative forms of payment and jeopardizing your health care in the process.

How is this possible? Why are some people bearing enormous health care costs while others have all of their bills paid by Medicare? Because Medicare doesn't cover custodial care if it is the only kind of care you need. Custodial care essentially includes assistance with basic activities of daily living, like walking, transferring, toileting, eating, bathing and grooming. It may also include assistance with oxygen, medications, insulin shots and caring for colostomy or bladder catheters. So when seniors need help getting in and out of bed or walking or bathing; help finding their way to the bathroom or taking their medicine or eating; help remembering how to sit down or drink water; when seniors are at their most vulnerable, and need the most care, our health care system abandons them.

What happened to John F. Kennedy's vision for universal medical insurance for all aged Americans?[7] The Medicare program was supposed to be there for all seniors regardless of their health care needs. Instead, it has shrunk to exclude those afflicted with the most devastating illnesses – even though they paid into the Medicare system since its inception. It doesn't make sense but it's true. If you need heart surgery, chemotherapy, a hip replacement: Medicare pays. If you have Alzheimer's disease, severe dementia, or are completely bedridden: Medicare does not pay. It's like the diagnosis lottery, where certain illnesses are covered and others are not. How is that fair?

Bottom Line: If you can't get better, Medicare no longer cares about you.

This is better illustrated by the visual on the following page, which Attorney Rick Law, Chicago's premier elder law attorney, has titled "*The Elder Care Journey.*" We prefer to call it "The Hi-Jacking of the American Retiree"

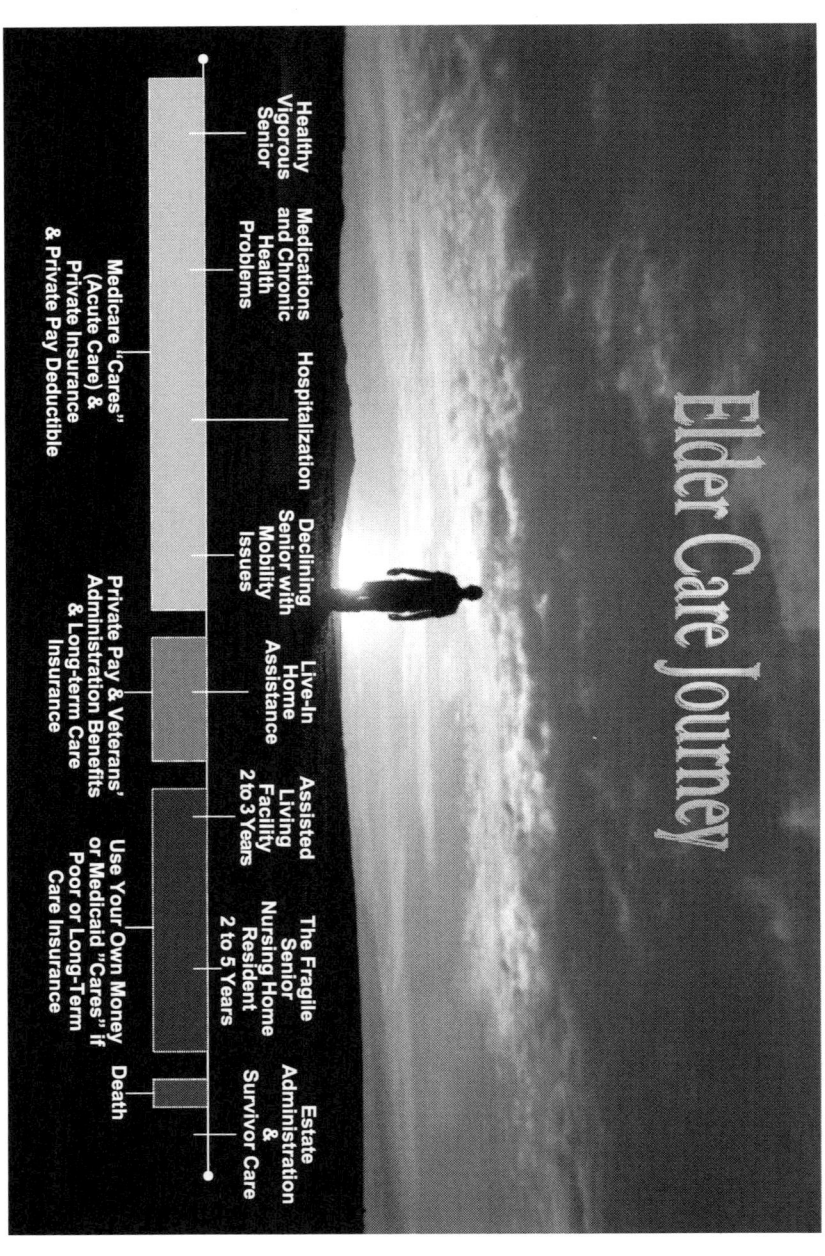

The Elder Care Journey starts with the healthy, vigorous senior. He may still be working or have recently retired, and is active in family or community life. He may take some medication, and may eventually develop chronic health problems like diabetes or heart disease. He may face hospitalizations or surgeries, and may ultimately become a declining senior with mobility issues. Throughout this stage of his health care, Medicare does a really good job of paying most of the bills. Whatever Medicare doesn't cover, supplemental health insurance usually makes up the difference.

Now, we don't mean to minimize or ignore the struggles of the countless seniors who find themselves in the donut hole, forced to spend astronomical amounts of their own money on pharmacy bills. But apart from inadequate prescription coverage, the majority of all acute health care costs are being paid in full by Medicare and supplemental health insurance.

This is well illustrated by the following example. If you're one of those people who have trouble sleeping, you may have seen one of those late night ads for the Scooter Store. These commercials are really compelling, because they essentially say, "Hey, seniors, if we can't get Medicare or your insurance to cover the cost of your scooter…we'll give it to you for free!" Isn't that amazing? They have got to be really confident that Medicare is going to pay for these scooters or they could never make that kind of an offer on television. They'd go broke if they did! But because they know that Medicare does such a great job paying for active seniors with mobility problems, they can afford to make that claim to thousands of people. When we're looking at an offer that good, we know that Medicare truly cares about seniors at this stage of the Elder Care Journey.

And with that kind of commitment by Medicare, it's easy for seniors to get comfortable thinking that Medicare will be there to pay all of their long-term care bills. So where does the hi-jacking come in? Right when you step over into the next phase of the journey. Because if your mobility issues worsen to the point where you need some in-home assistance, which can cost $15-$20 per hour, Medicare stops caring about you. Maybe you live alone, or your spouse is frail and can't lift you, and you need to hire someone to come to your home and help you get out of bed, or help you bathe or get dressed, or check your insulin levels, or stay with you for an hour so your spouse can have a little break. Medicare doesn't care. They aren't paying anymore and you have to pay for that yourself. Wonder what JFK would think about that?

And what happens when you go further along this journey and your health declines and it's not safe for you to stay in your own home anymore? Maybe you need to move to an assisted living facility where there are no stairs, and you can get more care in a safe environment with people to monitor and check on you; make sure you don't wander away; make sure you eat and take your medicines on time. Well Medicare doesn't care about that either. The cost at this stage can be $3,000 to $5,000 per month, depending on how much assistance you need. Who can afford to pay that bill every month without going broke in a hurry?

What becomes of the fragile senior whose health care needs require 24-hour skilled care? This may be your spouse with advanced Alzheimer's or dementia, who must be monitored at all times for her own safety; or your husband who is bedridden and can no longer communicate. Does Medicare care at all about your nursing home bill, which on average costs about $7,000 to $8,000 every month? You guessed it – it doesn't care at all. At those prices, it is very easy to see how a family's entire life savings can be wiped out in a matter of months.

Although another government program called Medicaid (addressed in detail in the next chapter) may assist you with your nursing home bills, you won't get any help until you have spent most of your own money first. That's right – the government will force you to spend so much of your own money, that by the time help arrives you may be left with almost nothing, despite the fact that you've paid taxes and social security all these years. Unless you have a plan, the government has a plan for you – go broke and then we will help you!

As you study the Elder Care Journey, it's easy to see how the cost of long-term care is truly the biggest financial threat (and the biggest Money Snatcher) faced by middle and upper-middle-class senior citizens today.

CHAPTER TWO

MEDICAID - A WOLF IN SHEEP'S CLOTHING

So where can you turn for help when Medicare turns its back on you?

Most turn to Medicaid, which is a government program designed to pay the health care expenses of the *impoverished*. That's right, when your government health insurance plan (Medi<u>care</u>) turns its back on you the next available option is Medi<u>caid</u>, a government program that won't help you at all until you are broke. Medicaid is misunderstood on many counts. Because of the similarity in names, it is often confused with Medicare. Medicare is your government health insurance. It is run by the federal government and is supplemented with your private health insurance. Medicare, as you now know, cannot be trusted or relied on to pay for long-term care. The most Medicare will cover in a nursing situation is "up to" one hundred days of care. But don't count on it – because it may cut you off much earlier.

And when Medicare turns its back on you, you are forced to turn to another government program to help you pay for long-term nursing home costs. That program is Medicaid. Medicaid is a government program that provides financial assistance to seniors to pay for nursing home costs and a limited amount of home health care. The greatest share of nursing home residents - currently about two-thirds - pay their skilled nursing home bill with money from Medicaid.[8] While Medicaid is a federal program, it is administered by each State, often with very conflicting, confusing and inconsistent results. This is probably why the National Academy of Elder Law Attorneys (NAELA) has referred to Medicaid as one of the most complex laws of the United States.[9] While Federal Medicaid guidelines must be followed, each state has its own version of Medicaid, with its own set of rules. This can and does make obtaining Medicaid approval a very tricky and unpredictable process. Rules vary from state to state, and are often interpreted differently even among counties within the same state. (It is important to note that the location of the nursing home, and not the patient's initial residency, determines which State rules govern the Medicaid application).

No matter what state they are in, one thing remains constant: Remember John and Mary? If Mary turns to Medicaid for help with John's nursing home bill, chances are she won't get any help from the government until she has blown through at least half or more of their own money first. But Mary is desperate. Medicare has abandoned her husband, and so has his supplemental health insurance. And when you have no place else to turn, you will take whatever help you can get – no matter the cost. If only John and Mary had planned ahead they could have kept the money they worked a lifetime to save. Because they didn't get their own plan in place before John got sick, they are now at the mercy of the government, and will be forced to follow the state's plan instead.

TAKE A TRIP DOWN MEDICAID LANE
How the Government's Plan Really Works

So what happens when you need Medicaid to help pay your nursing home bill? To qualify for Medicaid nursing home coverage, an applicant must meet three eligibility tests.[10]

- Category test: Applicants must be at least one of the following: age 65 or older, disabled, or blind.

For most seniors needing help to pay nursing home expenses, meeting this test is not a problem.

- Income test: In most states, the applicant is required to "spend-down" the majority of their monthly income (minus a small personal needs allowance) as a co-pay to the nursing home. In "income-cap" states, if the applicant's monthly income is greater than $2,022, they will be disqualified from receiving Medicaid (although planning opportunities may exist to allow eligibility under certain conditions).

- Asset test: The Medicaid applicant is allowed to own only minimal assets (in most states this is capped at $2,000 for an individual). The spouse of the applicant is generally allowed to keep ½ of the total countable assets up to $109,560. The spouse will always be able to keep the first $21,912, and in some states may be permitted to keep the first $109,560, even if that represents more than ½ of the couple's total assets.[11]

Regardless of the applicable income and asset limits, Medicaid will not help you in any state until you prove that you are financially needy. You will be required to follow strict guidelines regarding assets and income. The rules vary if you are single or married. Certain assets are exempt, meaning Medicaid won't consider them resources available for payment and won't count them toward your allowable asset limit. Most assets, however, are not exempt and will be counted against you for purposes of determining your Medicaid eligibility.

EXEMPT ASSETS (What you can keep)

In addition to the asset limits discussed above, certain assets, regardless of value, will be considered exempt by Medicaid and not counted toward your permissible asset limits.

An applicant and their spouse may typically keep their personal belongings, such as clothing, jewelry and furniture, and those items will not be included when Medicaid calculates total assets. If an applicant owns an original Renoir or other valuable artwork insured for several hundred thousand dollars, we suspect he may encounter some difficulty classifying it as exempt under the household goods exemption; but for the most part, furniture, home décor, appliances and electronics will be considered exempt.

One automobile is exempt, regardless of value, even if you can't drive it. However, Medicaid does require that the vehicle be used for transportation of the Medicaid applicant or household family member. Again, you'll be hard pressed to convince Medicaid that a classic Rolls Royce that is only driven to car shows once a year is an exempt asset. Some folks do get creative and purchase expensive cars (often referred to as "Medicaid Cadillacs") to try to maximize savings under the automobile exemption. But most seniors will probably derive more financial benefit by utilizing other money-saving strategies, such as those outlined in Chapter Eight.

Your principal residence is typically exempt while you are alive, even if you are living in the nursing home, provided that your home is located in the same state where you are applying for Medicaid. Most states have an "intent to return" rule, which presumes that the Medicaid applicant's intention, no matter how unrealistic, is to eventually move back home. Some states, however, like Ohio, will force a single person to put their house up for sale within 13 months of entering the nursing home. The money gained from the sale of the house is not exempt and will be included in the countable assets of the applicant. After February 8, 2006, the effective date of the Deficit Reduction Act, an applicant's home in all states is exempt only if the equity in the home is under $500,000. Equity above $500,000 is not exempt and will be considered a countable resource (unless dependents reside in the home). Homes of married couples are treated differently. In all states, if the spouse (or dependent family member) of the Medicaid applicant resides in the home, it is considered an exempt asset regardless of the value or equity in the home. But this is a tricky exemption. If the community spouse (the spouse at home) sells the house, she could turn an exempt asset into a non-exempt countable asset, and the sales proceeds may be considered available resources that are subject to a Medicaid spend down.

We feel compelled to warn you - because the Government will never make this clear to you – that **your house is never really safe when you are on Medicaid.** If the deed to your house is in your name or your spouse's name (or both) and one of you is receiving Medicaid, Medicaid can come back and snatch your house when the Medicaid recipient dies. You'll learn more about this secret money-snatcher called *estate recovery* in our discussion on hidden medical taxes in Chapter Seven.

CAUTION: **Adding your children's names to your real estate deed does nothing to protect your home from being snatched later by Medicaid. In fact, adding anyone else's name to your deed can have devastating consequences irrespective of Medicaid. In Chapter**

Four, we'll give you the real scoop on why this big mistake is one you could avoid at all costs – because if you don't, it can really cost YOU!!!

Burial plots are exempt assets, as are pre-paid funerals of the Medicaid applicant - and his or her spouse. But in order to be exempt, a pre-paid funeral contract must be irrevocable and unassignable. If you can change your mind and revoke your contract with the funeral home, or cash it out and get your money back, then your pre-paid funeral contract will not be considered an exempt asset and you will be required to cash it out and spend that money down. While pre-paying funerals is popular "spend-down" advice from most Medicaid caseworkers, in reality planning a funeral in advance for a loved one who just entered a nursing home is an extremely difficult task. Because this exemption comes with its share of risk, both emotionally and financially, an alternative to the traditional pre-paid funeral is discussed in Chapter Eight.

Medicaid in all states considers a small amount of your life insurance as anexempt asset. Typically, group policies through your employer have no cash or surrender value and are therefore exempt (because you have no way to turn those policies into available dollars to pay the nursing home bill). Term policies having no cash value are also exempt. Likewise, if the total *face*  value of your life insurance policies is less than $1,500, those policies are exempt. But if the total *face* value of all life insurance policies in your name exceeds $1,500, those policies are not exempt, and the surrender value in those policies will be considered available resources to pay the nursing home. You may be forced to spend the cash in those policies and lose the death benefits.

Suppose you have a life insurance policy with a $100,000 death benefit and present surrender value of $23,000. You have been paying the premium on this policy for years because you place a high value on passing this money on to your spouse or children when you die. But if you apply for Medicaid, the state will view that policy as a $23,000 resource available to pay the nursing home.

That life insurance policy will be treated no differently than $23,000 in your bank account. Before Medicaid will help with your nursing home bill, you will be forced to cash that policy out and lose the death benefit, turning a $100,000 future benefit into $23,000 cash that must be spent down. This can be especially devastating to your spouse if her biggest means of support after your death is supposed to be that big life insurance policy that you've been paying for year after year. How can you tell if your life insurance is at risk? Check out the name of the owner on the policy. If it's **you**, the policy is not safe.

Are you starting to see how Medicaid - the program most seniors turn to for help - is actually a wolf, a real money snatcher, in sheep's clothing? But don't despair. Read on and you will discover that there is a better way to own your home and your life insurance to make them truly exempt assets that will be protected when disability strikes.

NON-EXEMPT ASSETS
(What You Must Spend)

Any assets not listed above are generally not exempt, which means Medicaid will include them when calculating your total assets and consider them as available resources to pay your nursing home bill. All of your CDs, money market accounts, IRAs, 401(k)s, checking and savings accounts, stocks, bonds, most annuities, second homes and investment properties (virtually everything else) will be considered countable resources that can disqualify you from Medicaid benefits unless they are spent down.

SINGLE APPLICANTS

In all states, single and married persons are treated differently by Medicaid. In most states, a single person can have no more than $2,000 worth of assets to qualify for Medicaid. Let's take a look at how Medicaid treats a single applicant.

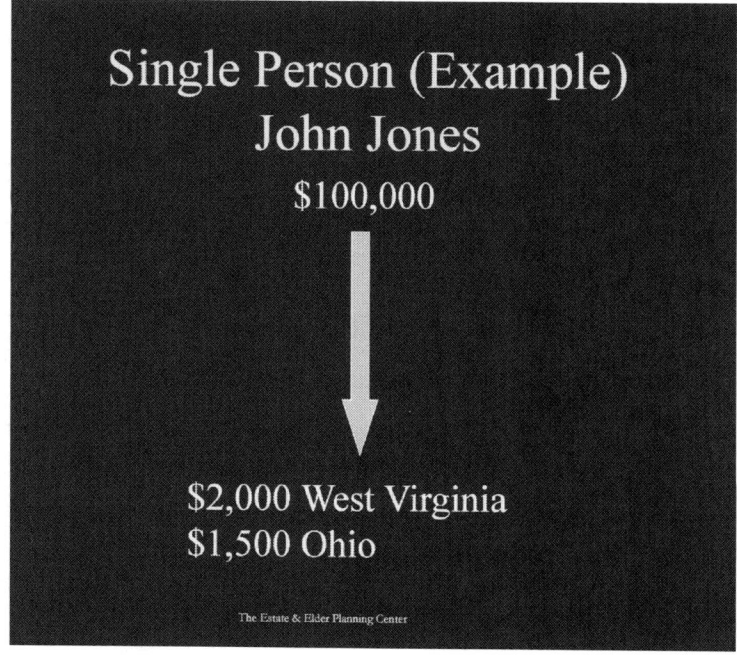

Single Person (Example)
John Jones
$100,000

$2,000 West Virginia
$1,500 Ohio

The Estate & Elder Planning Center

In our example, John Jones, a single man, lives in Ohio but is entering a nursing home in West Virginia. His total countable assets, including his bank accounts and his IRA, total $100,000. Like most states, before the State of West Virginia will help pay his nursing home bill, John will be forced to spend $98,000 of his own money first, leaving him with only $2,000. In terms of today's medical care costs, John Jones might as well have nothing. It is extremely important to remember that adding your children's names to your bank accounts does *not* protect those accounts from the nursing home. Medicaid follows a source of funds rule – if your child or other joint account holder can prove that they actually put money into the account, the portion of funds contributed by them will be excluded. So if John Jones put his daughter's name on his $30,000 savings account, the entire amount is still considered a countable asset unless he can prove that his daughter contributed her own money to that account. If she did, then her portion of that money will be considered exempt and the rest will be counted. But if the account is comprised solely of John's money, Medicaid will view all of the money in the joint bank account as a countable asset available to pay the nursing home - and will require John to spend all of that money before helping him with his nursing home bill.

What About Income??

When Medicaid starts to pay for a single applicant, that applicant will be forced to use virtually all of his income as his co-pay to the nursing home. In most states you are permitted to keep between $45.00-$60.00 per month for incidentals, like hair cuts, toiletries, or your favorite snacks. Other than this small monthly allowance, and whatever amount is needed to pay for supplemental health insurance premiums, a single person's entire pension, social security check, rental income - everything else - is gone. That's right: Before the government helps you with your long-term care expenses, they are going to snatch your income first. Without proper planning, a single person will essentially be broke before getting any help from Medicaid. And when you are out of money, you are out of options, and truly at the mercy of the government.

Remember, some states are considered "income cap" states, meaning that Medicaid will deny coverage to those whose income exceeds $2,022 (even by $1.00), although special planning opportunities may be available in certain circumstances to obtain eligibility despite excess income.

MARRIED APPLICANTS

Married couples are treated differently. Before reviewing a couple's assets to determine the "spend down" amount, Medicaid will establish a "snapshot date." A determination of the married couple's assets will be made on the date that the disabled spouse begins a continuous period of institutionalization. This could be the date the disabled spouse first enters the hospital, if the spouse is then immediately transferred from the hospital to a long-term care facility; otherwise, the snapshot date will generally be considered the first date of admission to the nursing home. If a nursing home admission is preceded by a lengthy period of hospitalization, the financial determination may be inaccurate when the Medicaid application is actually made. (For example, stock prices may have dropped or investment accounts may have lost value). But the snapshot date controls, and whichever day Medicaid determines is the official snapshot date will ultimately rule. The couple's financial picture on that date is the one Medicaid will use to determine approval (or denial) when the application is made.

In order to understand how the "spend-down" works for a married couple, you must first accept that in most states Medicaid will count virtually all of the couple's assets, regardless of whose name is on the account. Remember John and Mary? John's IRA, Mary's CD, their joint checking and savings accounts, all of their stocks, bonds, every account they own, is tallied up in one lump sum and counted as their total assets. A few states, like Pennsylvania, will allow Mary (the at-home spouse) to keep her IRA or other qualified retirement account. But in most states, the community spouse's IRA or other retirement account is included in the asset pool and will be required to be spent down. *A Word of Caution:* The exempt IRA can be totally lost by keeping the institutionalized spouse as a beneficiary of the account, because if the community spouse – the supposedly healthy spouse - dies first, the institutionalized spouse will inherit the IRA and it can all be lost to the nursing home.

Let's examine how Medicaid treats a married applicant.

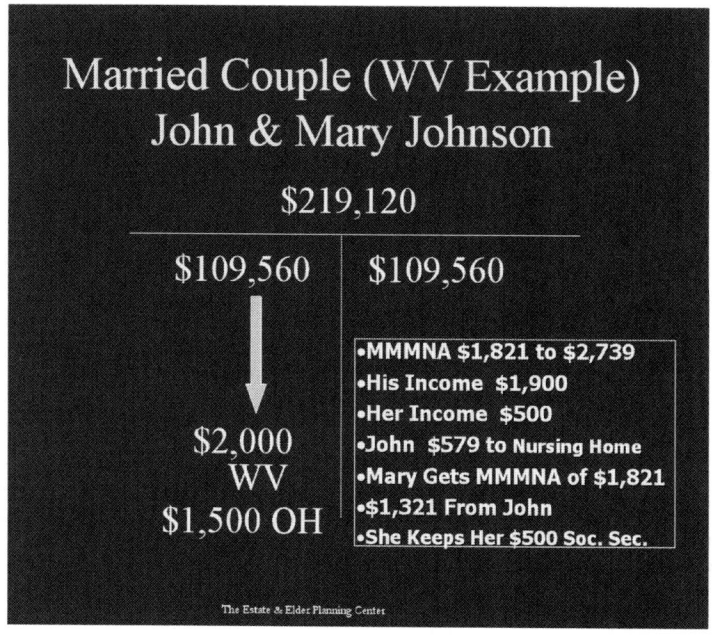

The chart above illustrates how Medicaid will treat John and Mary's assets and income when reviewing John's application for nursing home assistance. John, who is entering the nursing home, is referred to as the Institutionalized Spouse (IS). Mary, who is at home, is called the Community Spouse (CS). As discussed earlier, their house is exempt (for now).

John and Mary's total countable assets are $219,120. The first thing Medicaid will do is divide the total countable assets in half, allotting $109,560 to each spouse. John, who is in the nursing home, will be forced to spend all of his assets down to approximately $2,000 in most states. Mary will be permitted to keep her entire $109,560. The amount that Mary is allowed to keep is called her Community Spousal Resource Allowance, or CSRA. While it may appear that we used an odd number of total countable assets in the above example, we chose that number to emphasize an important Medicaid rule on the division of marital assets. Let's assume that John and Mary have total countable assets of $300,000. Again, Medicaid will divide the assets in half; this time allotting $150,000 to the institutionalized spouse (John) and $150,000 to the community spouse (Mary). John will still be required to spend his $150,000 down to $2,000 in most states. But Mary will not be permitted to keep all of her $150,000, because the most that a community spouse can keep is $109,560. That's right. The maximum

Community Spousal Resource Allowance (or CSRA) in all states s $109,560.[12] If John and Mary have $500,000, Mary is still allowed to keep only $109,560 as her CSRA. So regardless of how much money a married couple has, the maximum amount that the at-home spouse will be permitted to keep is $109,560, and the maximum amount that the institutionalized spouse can keep is approximately $2,000. The rest of the money must be spent down before Medicaid will help pay the nursing home bill. A different rule applies for married couples with a small amount of assets. In all states, a community spouse will always be permitted to keep the first $21,912, even if that represents more than half of the couple's total assets. And in a few states, a community spouse will always be allowed to keep the first $109,560, even if that amounts to more than half of their total assets, leaving much less to the institutionalized spouse to be spent on care.

It's easy to see how a married couple's savings can plummet to $111,560 in no time flat if disability strikes - snatching away in months what it took a lifetime to build.

Income Diversion

As previously discussed, single applicants will lose the bulk of their income to the nursing home in the form of their monthly co-pay. Like assets, the income of married couples is also treated differently. If a community spouse's gross income is below $1,821.25, Medicaid will permit the institutionalized applicant to give (or divert) a monthly allowance to his spouse to prevent her from becoming impoverished. This is referred to as the Minimum Monthly Maintenance Needs Allowance (MMMNA).[13] Medicaid permits an institutionalized person to divert as much of their income as needed to ensure that their at-home spouse receives the total MMMNA each month. (After all, the government doesn't want to see the community spouse on welfare when it is already being asked to pay the other spouse's nursing home expenses). The institutionalized person may also deduct a portion of their income for a dependent child living at home. A community spouse may request a fair hearing to determine whether they are eligible for an increase in the amount of income diverted (thereby increasing the MMMNA) if they can demonstrate a need for the additional income, up to the Maximum Monthly Maintenance Needs Allowance of $2,739.[14]

While the institutionalized spouse's income is all fair game, the community spouse is usually permitted to retain her income. If a community spouse is still working, or has a large monthly pension, she can typically keep all of her income and will not be required to contribute – or divert – one dime to the nursing home to help pay the cost of care for her spouse. Not only does this rule protect the wages and retirement earnings of a community spouse, it is especially important as it is the basis for most nursing home asset protection being done for married couples today.

THE DEFICIT REDUCTION ACT

It's easy to see how nursing home costs are an enormous money snatcher, draining your income and almost all of your assets! But so is Medicaid; because this government program turns its back on the frailest senior citizens in their greatest time of need, withholding assistance until they are essentially impoverished. And as you will learn in Chapter Six, once Medicaid does start paying a person's nursing home bills, that secret money snatcher called *estate recovery* can come back later and take their house away from their family after they die.

As of February 8, 2006, our government hijacked the senior population once again! That's the day The Deficit Reduction Act of 2005 (DRA) was signed into law......
and drastically changed the way our government treats disabled seniors needing nursing home care. This new law severely restricted the ability of senior citizens to transfer their assets, changing the "look-back" period from 3 years to 5 years. It also reduced home equity limits to $500,000, treating the excess equity as a countable resource available for payment.[15] The law essentially presumes that the elderly give money and property away to defraud the government and impermissibly obtain Medicaid benefits,

and therefore imposes harsh penalties for even innocent gifts to family or donations to churches and charities. *This law changed the starting date of all transfer penalties, moving it up to the date of application. The result:* **NO GIFTS ARE SAFE UNTIL FIVE YEARS PASS FROM THE DATE OF THE GIFT.** When the Medicaid application is filed, all assets transferred (gifted) within the preceding five years will be treated as if they were gifted on the date of application. This means that the period of ineligibility created by a gift (that used to start on the day the gift was made) doesn't start until you actually apply for Medicaid. It is important to note that gifts made *prior* to February 8, 2006 still fall under the old rules and will be treated by Medicaid as safe since 3 years have passed since the gift was made. Post DRA, you must gift with caution. Gifts that you make when you are healthy and not even remotely considering the possibility of future nursing home care can come back to haunt you – and severely compromise your health care – if you become disabled within the next five years.

The DRA also changed Medicaid's view of annuities, which used to be an easy way to turn countable assets into exempt income and protect the money from being spent on the nursing home. Commercially available, run of the mill annuities are no longer safe from inclusion as a countable resource. Unless your annuity conforms to the strict guidelines set forth by Medicaid (Medicaid

Qualifying Annuity) it will be treated like all other assets and will be subject to the spend - down.[16]

SPENDING DOWN

So you've been told by the Medicaid case worker that you have to "spend down" your assets. What can you spend the money on? A permissible (but not very desirable) choice is to pay the monthly nursing home expense. However, when the bill is $6,000 - $7,000 per month, your funds can be depleted very quickly. You can prepay funerals (provided the funeral contract is irrevocable and unassignable); you can pay for home repairs; pay off your debts, such as mortgages or credit card balances; or buy a new car (remember those Medicaid Cadillacs?) While some may choose to purchase expensive cars or install new kitchen cabinets, most people facing a loss of significant income and assets would rather preserve enough money to pay their bills rather than spending it on things they don't really need.

Within the Medicaid rules in every state, there are acceptable alternatives to spending down and losing all the money. But as with most things financial, there is one set of rules for the informed and another set of rules for the uninformed and misinformed. Everyone believes that they must "spend down" and lose all of their money because that is what they are told – by their friends and family, by folks at the coffee shop and beauty parlor, and by caseworkers at the local Medicaid office. To avoid a potential spend-down in the future, many folks mistakenly believe that they should just give all of their stuff to their kids now. In Chapter Four, we'll tell you why this is a bad idea, and how gifting can actually be hazardous to your health…and wealth!

The reality is there are numerous strategies that can be employed to save money and avoid becoming impoverished, even if you are facing an immediate nursing home crisis and have been told you must spend down. But the Government is never going to inform you of those money-saving techniques. And the Medicaid caseworkers are not permitted to give financial or estate planning guidance that could alleviate the harsh result created by spending down. It's up to **YOU** to get informed and take action to preserve your life savings. *BE WARNED:* Changes in Medicaid laws make asset protection planning more difficult every year. The clock is ticking, and **NOW** is the best time to devise and implement your game plan, *before* disability strikes.

In Chapter Eight we will share with you some of the methods that we have used to help our clients preserve assets and obtain health care benefits without going broke. The best strategy is to design a battle plan before you ever go to war. Early planning ensures that **YOU**, and not the government, are in charge. But don't try to go it alone, because when it comes to asset protection and Medicaid planning, one size definitely doesn't fit all. Be sure to seek advice from experienced professionals who can review your finances and legal documents to develop a specific plan that is just right for your unique situation. That's the best way to avoid falling victim to the most prevalent money-snatchers that plague senior citizens today; long-term care costs and the government programs designed to pay for them.

CHAPTER THREE

AID & ATTENDANCE PENSION BENEFIT

THE VA'S BEST KEPT SECRET

Millions of dollars are going unclaimed from the Veteran's Administration because Veterans are unaware that a benefit exists to help them pay for long-term care. It is called the Aid and Attendance Pension Benefit... the VA's best kept secret. Aging veterans who are in need of home health care, assisted living, or even nursing home care may be eligible for a monthly stipend to pay long term care bills for themselves and their spouses. That's right: Government money is available for veterans, their spouses, and their widows to help pay their long-term health care bills... and it's all *tax-free!* Unfortunately, most Veterans don't take advantage of this benefit because they have no idea that it exists. Little is known about this financial assistance program because the VA hasn't spread the word about these special healthcare benefits, and has imposed strict rules regarding who is actually permitted to help veterans obtain them. Only Federal and State

VA employees and authorized representatives of Veterans Service Organizations like the VFW and American Legion can help veterans file for benefits. So can lawyers and agents who are accredited by the VA.[17] But most lawyers (even elder law attorneys) are in the dark when it comes to this benefit.

Most people think that veterans' benefits are only available to those who were wounded or disabled while serving in the Armed Forces. While those service-connected pensions are available to veterans who were injured during a time of war, the Aid and Attendance benefit is different because it is earmarked for aging veterans with long-term care needs. The VA considers this a special monthly pension that can help pay expenses associated with Alzheimer's, Parkinson's, dementia, MS or a host of other diseases that can cause a veteran to become homebound or need the ongoing assistance of another.

The wartime veteran has earned possible eligibility for this assistance because they served our country, even if their current disability is *not* connected to their military service. This is not a service-connected pension, meaning there is no requirement of a wartime injury. Seniors who served our country during a time of war and are now in failing health from illnesses like Alzheimer's Disease, Parkinson's, or stroke,

may qualify for significant financial assistance to help pay health care bills instead of struggling to make ends meet or failing to hire much needed help at home. Money is also available for ailing spouses and widows of veterans.

A single or widowed veteran with no dependents who is in need of regular aid and attendance may receive a maximum annual pension benefit of $19,736, or $1,644 per month. If the veteran is married or has a dependent child, the maximum pension is $23,396, or $1,949 per month. If the veteran's spouse is in need of care, the veteran is still able to receive the same maximum benefit of $1,949 to pay for her care. If a surviving spouse of a veteran is in need of regular aid and attendance, the maximum pension benefit is $12,681, or $1,056 per month. If the surviving spouse has a dependent child the maximum pension is $15,128, or $1,260 per month. Each additional dependent will increase the pension $2,016 annually - or $168 per month. To be in need of regular aid and attendance, the veteran or spouse must be permanently and totally disabled and (1) a patient in a nursing home; (2) blind, or nearly blind; or (3) needing the regular aid and attendance of another person to perform basic activities of daily living, such as dressing, bathing, and transferring.

Special Pension Rates
Paid to Veterans age 65 or older OR Permanently and Totally Disabled[18]

SITUATION	MAXIMUM ANNUAL PENSION RATE	MAXIMUM MONTHLY CHECK
Veteran in need of regular aid and attendance (single, no dependents)	$19,736	$1,644
Veteran in need of regular aid and attendance (married or with dependent child)	$23,396	$1,949
Veteran with spouse who is in need of regular aid and attendance	$23,396	$1,949
Widow of a Veteran, needing regular aid and attendance	$12,681	$1,056

This is NOT a handout or charity – after all, our veterans risked their lives to protect our country, and the least we can do is support them in their time of need. The maximum monthly benefit can provide significant help paying the long-term care costs of veterans and their surviving spouses who are homebound or in a care facility. And these benefits can play a huge role in keeping a loved one at home and out of the nursing home. Wouldn't it be nice if the government made that clear?

Veterans who are injured during wartime service are often treated like employees filing for workers' compensation. They are typically subjected to the VA's rating system, and their disability is rated as a percentage. For example, VA examiners may rate someone as low as 10% or as high as 100% disabled. The injured veteran receives a benefits check based on this rating, and not based on need. Unlike that type of service-connected pension, no disability ratings are associated with the Aid and Attendance benefit, which is a non-service connected special monthly pension benefit. Wartime veterans (and their surviving spouses) whose disabilities are *not* caused by their service become eligible for the special monthly pension benefit when they are over 65 years of age; are permanently disabled and unable to work; are homebound; or need the regular aid and attendance of another – whether at home, in assisted living, or in a nursing home.[19]

So what's the catch? There are strict eligibility requirements, and understanding the specific rules of the VA can make all the difference in whether or not you receive an award. Read on and you will learn the secrets for unlocking this hidden government benefit.

SERVICE REQUIREMENT

The service requirement for this VA benefit is as follows: The veteran must have served 90 consecutive days of active duty, at least one day of which was during a period of war. This doesn't mean they had to have served overseas, or been on the front lines…they just had to serve, either at home or abroad, during that time frame. Even if the Veteran served in a lesser-known area of the military, they may be eligible for this benefit. Take a look at the list below. In addition to active duty vets from traditional areas of the armed services (Army, Navy, Air Force, Marines) these groups also meet the service requirement for the Aid and Attendance benefits.

Veterans who served 90 consecutive days active duty (with at least one day during a time of war) and received an honorable discharge by the Secretary of Defense from any of the following service groups[20], meet the active duty service requirement for the Aid and Attendance benefit:

• Recipients of the Medal of Honor	• Women Air Force Service Pilots (WASPs)
• Civilian crewmen of certain U.S. Coast and Geodetic Survey vessels between 12/7/41 and 8/15/45	• U.S. civilians of the American Field Service who served overseas under U.S. armies and U.S. army groups in WWII
• WWI Signal Corps Female Telephone Operators Unit	• American merchant marines in oceangoing service during WWII
• WWI Engineer Field Clerks	• Women's Army Auxiliary Corps (WAAC)
• U.S. civilian employees of American Airlines who served overseas in contract with the Air Transport Command between 12/14/41 and 8/14/45	• U.S. civilian flight crew and aviation ground support of Consolidated Vultee Aircraft Corp. who served overseas between 12/14/41 and 8/14/45
• Female clerical employees of the Quartermaster Corps serving with the American Expeditionary Forces in WWI	• U.S. civilian flight crew and aviation ground support of TWA who served overseas between 12/14/41 and 8/14/45
• Male civilian ferry pilots	• Reconstruction aides and dietitians of WWI
• Civilian employees of Pacific naval air bases who actively participated in defense of Wake Island during WWII	• Honorably discharged members of the American Volunteer Guard, Eritrea Service Command, between 6/21/42 and 3/31/43
• Quartermaster Corps members of the Keswick crew on Corregidor during WWII	• Civilian Navy IFF radar technicians who served in combat areas of the Pacific during WWII

• Wake Island defenders from Guam	• Guam Combat Patrol
• U.S. civilians who participated in the defense of Bataan U.S. merchant seamen who served on block ships in support of Operation Mulberry in the WWII invasion of Normandy	• U.S. civilian flight crew and aviation ground support of Braniff Airways who served overseas in the North Atlantic between 2/26/42 to 8/14/45
• Chamorro and Carolina former native police who received military training in the Donnal area of central Saipan and were placed under command of Lt. Casino of the 6th Provisional Military Police Battalion to accompany U.S. Marines on active, combat patrol from 8/19/45 to 9/2/45	• The operational Analysis Group of the Office of Scientific Research and Development, Office of Emergency Management, which served overseas with the U.S. Army Air Corps from 12/7/41 through 8/15/45
• U.S. civilian flight crew and aviation ground support of Northwest Airlines who served over- seas between 12/14/41 and 8/14/45	• Honorably discharged members of the Alaska Territorial Guard during WWII
• Members of the American Volunteer Group (Flying Tigers) who served between 12/7/41 and 8/14/45	• U.S. civilian female employees of the U.S. Army Nurse Corps who served in the defense of Bataan and Corregidor from 1/2/42 to 2/3/45
	• Civilian personnel assigned to OSS secret in- telligence
Army, Navy, Air Force, & Marines	

Even if a veteran is a member of one of the groups listed in the service requirements chart, his actual date of service is also a critical component of this benefit's criteria. In order to qualify for this benefit, the veteran must have served during the specific time frames set forth by the VA to be considered "wartime service." Now remember, the veteran must have been honorably discharged, and must have served *90 consecutive days of active duty, including at least ONE DAY in one of the following date ranges*[21]:

Official Dates for Periods of War*

Mexican Border	May 9, 1916 to April 5, 1917
World War I	April 6, 1917 to November 11, 1918 -Or until April 1, 1920 if served in Russia
World War II	December 7, 1941 to December 31, 1946
Korean War	June 27, 1950 to January 31, 1955
Vietnam War	August 5, 1964 to May 7, 1975 -Or beginning February 28, 1961 if served in Vietnam
Persian Gulf War	August 2, 1990 to ? (date not yet determined)

*Information concerning a veteran's date of service can be found on his discharge paper identified as a DD-214. Check the dates of both entering and leaving the service, and check for an honorable or general discharge. If you cannot locate your discharge papers, contact a Veterans Service Organization, or a qualified specialist, for assistance.

DISABILITY REQUIREMENT

In order to qualify for the Aid and Attendance benefit, the veteran (or spouse) must be permanently and totally disabled. Meeting that disability requirement is not as difficult as it sounds. If you are at least 65 years old, the VA automatically presumes that you are disabled. Also, if the veteran or spouse is currently in a skilled nursing home, or is receiving Social Security disability benefits, they will easily meet this requirement. Otherwise, the veteran must submit medical records and a physician's statement to substantiate the existence of a disability. The veteran must provide proof that he is unable to work as a result of a disability or illness, and that the disability or illness is reasonably expected to continue throughout his lifetime. Even if a disability is established, the veteran will still be required to submit medical evidence demonstrating a need for the regular aid and attendance of another in order to receive this benefit.[22]

For aging veterans with failing health who are in need of long-term care, it is relatively easy to satisfy the disability prong of the VA's qualification test. Unfortunately, the other hurdles aren't as easy.

Being considered a wartime veteran does not automatically guarantee you will receive this benefit. Fighting for our country isn't even half the battle. How does the VA dole out these benefits, and when are wartime veterans able to receive them? The program is based on actual financial need for assistance, which means there are strict income and asset limitations. In determining a veteran's financial need for the benefit, the maximum annual pension rate (MAPR) available per veteran is calculated by taking into consideration some of the following factors:

- Gross household income available to pay expenses;
- Gross household assets - savings and other money available from IRAs, CDs, cash value life insurance, stocks, bonds, annuities, rented real estate, vacation homes, and all other investments;
- Life expectancy of the veteran (to determine how long the veteran may live and have to pay medical expenses); and
- The cost of ongoing medical expenses that are not covered by Medicare, employee benefits, or other insurance (these are called unreimbursed medical expenses, or UME's).[23]

Net "Income for Veterans Administration Purposes" (IVAP) is what is used to calculate how much, if any, pension money will be given to a veteran. Each *category* of need—such as housebound veteran, nursing home resident veteran, or veteran's spouse—has a *maximum* amount of pension dollars available per claimant (listed in the Special Pension Rates table. Because there is a maximum annual pension rate (MAPR) for each category, no one can receive a pension for more than the maximum set amount —*regardless of actual need.*)

INCOME REQUIREMENT

In order to be eligible for the Aid and Attendance Pension Benefit, the veteran must meet the strict income requirement set forth by the VA. Those who are "in the know" understand that gross income isn't the correct amount used in determining eligibility. Unfortunately, many people mistakenly believe that only low-income candidates are eligible for this benefit. That is simply not true. Remember: The real income utilized for the Aid and Attendance benefit is called your IVAP, or Income for VA Purposes. There are many veterans with higher income who also have high long-term care costs. Those veterans are equally entitled to the Aid and Attendance Benefit.

Understanding how the calculation works is critical to unlocking this valuable benefit. In order to determine the IVAP, you must start with the total gross monthly income of the veteran, spouse, and other dependents living in the household. You are then permitted to subtract all of the *unreimbursed* medical expenses (UMEs) being paid out each month. UME's include things like supplemental health insurance premiums, prescription bills, co-pays for physician's visits and hospital bills, home health care providers, and assisted living and nursing home bills. You are not permitted to subtract mortgage payments, utility bills, or other household expenses. The remaining balance is considered your true monthly income for VA purposes and is the actual income figure to be used when determining benefit eligibility.[24]

Again, the VA will subtract from your income what it considers "Unreimbursed Medical Expenses" – that is, what you and your spouse pay out of your pockets every month – to determine your net income for benefits consideration. This is a *key factor* to help you determine if you qualify for a pension.

The formula the VA uses to calculate your true income is demonstrated below:

Wartime Veteran & Spouse (if any) Gross household income

Minus:	Unreimbursed medical expenses (UME)

Equals:	Net income for Veterans Administration purposes (IVAP)

It's important to note that household annual income includes everything that is earned by the veteran, as well as the veteran's spouse and all dependents or others living in the household. From that total income amount, you may then subtract your un-reimbursed medical expenses (UMEs), which include things like Medicare costs and co-payments, pharmacy bills, supplemental health insurance premiums, home health care costs, the cost of assisted living facilities or in-home caretakers and even nursing home bills. You may also deduct payments to family members who are assisting with your care, but proceed with caution: Payments to family members will only be deductible from income when made pursuant to properly drafted caregiver agreements.

The following tables illustrate numerous other medical expenses that qualify:

Medicare Premiums Deducted from Social Security

Supplementary Medical Insurance Under Medicare Part B

Abdominal Supports

Acupuncture Service

Ambulance Hire

Anesthetist

Assisted Living Medical Bills

Arch Supports

Artificial Limbs

Back Supports

Braces

Cardiographs

Chiropractor

Convalescent Home (for medical treatment only)

Crutches

Dental Services

Dentures

Dermatologist

Eyeglasses

X rays

Food or Beverages Prescribed by Doctor for Treatment of Illness

Gynecologist

Hearing Aids & Batteries

Home Health Services

Hospital Expenses

Insulin Treatment

Insurance Premium 9medical)

Invalid Chair

Lab Tests

Lip Reading Lessons (in connection with disability)

Neurologist

Nursing Services

Occupational Therapist

Ophthalmologist

Optician

Optometrist

Oral Surgery

Osteopath

Pediatrician

Physical Examinations

Physician

Physical Therapy

Podiatrist

Prescriptions & Drugs

Psychiatrist

Psychoanalyst

Psychologist

Psychotherapy

Radium Therapy

Sacroiliac Belt

Seeing Eye Dog

Speech Therapist

Surgeon

Surgeon

Telephone / Teletype
For Deaf

Transportation Expenses
(.20 cents per mile)

Vaccines

Vitamins Prescribed
by Doctor

Wheelchairs

Whirlpool Baths for
Medical Purposes

**NOTE: Most
medical expenses
must be prescribed
by a physician to be
deductible from gross
income for VA benefit
qualification purposes x**

So you see, depending on your income and medical expenses, you may qualify for Aid and Attendance benefits – even if your gross monthly income *seems* too high. The income you need to be looking at is your gross income minus all of the UME's, which gives you your true income for VA purposes (IVAP).

After the VA determines your IVAP, it moves on to the next prong of the financial test – your assets.

ASSET REQUIREMENT

When it comes to the asset test, somebody really needs to call rumor control! There is a myth floating around concerning the amount of money you are allowed to keep and still qualify for the Aid & Attendance Pension Benefit. Many people are mistakenly advised that a single person can have $50,000 and married couples $80,000 and still qualify for the Veteran's benefit. In fact, asset limits are determined on a case-by-case basis, and relying on inaccurate numbers when applying for the benefit can cause significant, and unnecessary, delay in receiving your award. When viewing your net worth the VA will take into consideration your income, cost of care, life expectancy and number of dependents. Certain items are exempt, like your house and car, and life insurance that has no cash value. Liquid assets such as cash, stocks, bonds, IRA's,

401(k)'s, money market accounts, mutual funds, most annuities, and all other investments will be considered by the VA in determining your financial need for the benefit.

The following example will better illustrate how this benefit works:

Case History
Daniel Day, Veteran

Social Security	$1,000
Assisted Living Cost	$3,000 per month
Net Income	-$2,000 per month

Assets $40,000 - Gone in 20 months

Potential Benefit $1,644 per month
@$356/mo, $40,000 lasts 9 years

The Estate & Elder Planning Center

In this simplified example, Daniel Day is a WWII veteran who currently resides in an assisted living facility. He has some trouble getting around on his own, and requires help with bathing, dressing and taking his medications.

While he requires assistance with activities of daily living, he doesn't need 24-hour skilled care and is not a candidate for a nursing home. Mr. Day is comfortable at this facility, and while of course he would rather be home, he is safer living at the facility where his basic health care needs are being met.

His total monthly income is $1,000, and his cost at the assisted living facility is $3,000 per month. So every month he is short $2,000 to pay the assisted living bill. Mr. Day has $40,000 in the bank, and each and every month he has to write a check from his savings to pay the difference to the assisted-living facility. He cannot turn to Medicaid for help with the assisted living bill because Medicaid does not pay for assisted living facilities. Remember, Medicaid only pays for 24-hour skilled nursing care and some limited home care. Yes, that is correct. Our government will pay a $7,000 per month nursing home bill, but will not pay a $3,000 per month assisted living bill! So what is Mr. Day going to do? He has to spend all of his money on his care, and at this rate, his money will run out in less than two years. What will he do when all of his money is gone? Without another option, Mr. Day will be forced to turn to Medicaid at that time, and may be forced to move to a nursing home where he does not belong.

Does Mr. Day have another option besides spending all of his money and then moving to a nursing home? Enter the

VA Aid and Attendance Pension Benefit! Because Mr. Day served his country during a time of war, is over the age of 65 and is disabled, he is eligible for $1,644 per month... tax-free! When he adds that benefit amount to his monthly income of $1,000, his monthly shortage is now only $356, which means his money will now last him almost nine years. It's easy to see that this benefit is a wonderful way to honor the military service of our veterans who sacrificed for this country, and help those veterans in their greatest time of need.

Let's see how this benefit can also be a Godsend for a married couple:

Case History
Mr. & Mrs. Knight
Veteran, World War II – Lives at home

Assets	$60,000
Social Security	$1,300 & $600 ($1900)
Unreimbursed Medical Expenses:	
Home health	-$2,150
Medications	-$700
Health Insurance	-$300
Net Income	-$1,250 (IVAP)
Potential Benefit	$1,949 per month
Widow's Benefit	$1,056 per month

The Estate & Elder Planning Center

Mr. Knight is a married WWII veteran who is in declining health. Because he is experiencing serious health problems, he requires a great deal of assistance with his activities of daily living, medications, and overall health care. In order to stay at home with his wife, he utilizes home health care services that cost $2,150 every month. Added to his other unreimbursed medical expenses, the home health care bill will quickly overwhelm this couple's finances. Mr. and Mrs. Knight currently have $60,000 in liquid assets, and their combined total monthly income is $1,900. Mrs. Knight might mistakenly believe – or be told- that her monthly household income of $1,900 is too high to qualify for the Aid and Attendance benefit. But remember- the IVAP is what counts. So let's see how this works.

*Mr. Knight can subtract all of the unreimbursed medical expenses from the total household income, including $300 for supplemental health insurance premiums, $700 for prescription bills, and $2,150 for home health care services… to arrive at the true income for VA purposes, which is **minus** $1,250. They actually have a <u>negative</u> income for VA purposes! Now, because their IVAP is below zero, Mr. Knight qualifies for the maximum tax-free benefit available to a married veteran, which is $1,949 per month. Their $60,000 can remain in savings and Mr. Knight can continue to get the care he needs, right where he wants to be…at home.*

It's important to note that if Mrs. Knight were the one who became disabled and needed the home health services, Mr. Knight could still obtain the full benefit to pay for his wife's health care. And if Mr. Knight then passes away, Mrs. Knight could continue to receive the widow's pension of $1,056 per month.

BEWARE THE MEDICAID TIME BOMB!

If a Veteran or his spouse has assets or income greater than what is allowed by the VA rules, they are not automatically disqualified from obtaining this benefit. Again, while this is a needs-based benefit, it is not designed to assist only low-income or impoverished veterans. Planning opportunities do exist to reduce assets and increase unreimbursed medical expenses; however, you must proceed with **CAUTION** when implementing such strategies for the Aid and Attendance benefit. Government rules can change without warning, and you must be fully informed before making any financial moves that might actually ruin your chances of getting any benefits. Worse, things can get quite tricky when trying to coordinate two very different government benefits – VA and Medicaid. These are two separate and distinct government programs, with different and often conflicting rules and regulations. Planning strategies that are perfectly acceptable to the VA (today) can destroy your eligibility for Medicaid in the future.

Why is that so important to know? Because even if a Veteran is receiving the maximum Aid and Attendance benefit of $1,949 a month, that would probably never be a sufficient amount to pay a future nursing home bill of $7,000 per month. So if the veteran's health declines to the point where he needs 24-hour skilled nursing home care, he may need to apply for a greater benefit amount than the VA provides. And when that veteran turns to the other government program designed to pay nursing home expenses (Medicaid) he or his family will be in for a very unpleasant surprise. Because if the veteran had transferred assets out of his name or had given money or property to his children to meet the asset test for VA benefits (which the VA currently permits), Medicaid will view those "planning strategies" as uncompensated transfers, or gifts. If five years hasn't passed since those gifts were made (remember that look-back period?) the veteran will be penalized for those transfers and Medicaid will refuse to pay his nursing home bill. Innocent gifts or transfers currently permitted by the VA can disqualify you from Medicaid if enough time hasn't passed. Certain gifts allowed by the VA are forbidden by Medicaid, and giving away assets can create large penalty periods and ineligibility for Medicaid benefits. When planning for a VA benefit you should always consider the possibility of a future need for Medicaid benefits. A proper understanding of the tricky coordination between these two programs is essential to safeguarding your future health care benefits. Otherwise, your VA planning strategies could be like ticking time bombs…and if your health declines, they could blow up in your face and jeopardize your ability to pay for your health care when you or your spouse need it the most.

BATTLING THROUGH THE RED TAPE

A final word about planning and filing for the VA benefit: **GET HELP!** Well, that is really two words…but very important ones. Most folks have no idea what it's like to deal with the Veterans' Administration. It is a huge agency and the application process can be overwhelming. One benefits consultant featured on ABC nightly news put it, "If you're gonna walk in the door and do it yourself, good luck…I'll see you in two years."[25]

After completing the long VA application forms for aid and attendance benefits, you must submit supporting documentation with the application. The VA is very particular about the manner and format of the documentation submitted. Medical records and physicians' reports must be provided to support your need for medical assistance and for help paying unreimbursed medical expenses (even if the general disability requirement is already met). The manner in which the VA requests and reviews this information can get confusing if you are not familiar with the rules. Also, the veteran is dependent on his doctors to complete their portion of the forms to the satisfaction of the VA. Busy doctors may not be willing to complete additional forms, or may be reluctant to phrase their reports in a manner that will ultimately satisfy the VA requirements. Even if you submit your physician evaluation forms, the VA may send you an Authorization to Release Medical Information, implying that more medical evidence is needed... but you may not know what records are missing. Once the claim is filed, months may pass before a response is received; and sending written correspondence may delay the process further because the VA will then be required to respond in writing to your inquiry. If your application is lost and re-submitted, you could end up with two claim numbers. This can create confusion and delay that leads to an even longer application process. When the VA acknowledges receipt of your application, their letter may include a list of items that were missing from your application. The letter may request additional medical information, but you may not know exactly what is needed. If you call the VA directly, you may become frustrated waiting to speak to the person who has been assigned to your claim.

When you receive the "VCAA Notice Response" form you'll be even more confused! The form contains two boxes. If you want 60 extra days to send in more information, check box one. If you want the VA to review your application and judge your claim immediately based only on what you have already sent in, check the other box. Without knowing whether you have actually sent all of the required information, it may be difficult to make an informed choice.

The key to filing the application for benefits in the most expeditious manner is to file what is considered a "ready to rate" claim. Understanding what the VA is really looking for, what they actually want to see, in what format, and at what time, can shave months – even years - off of the claims process. Get help and get informed before you file your application for Aid and Attendance benefits. Knowing the rules and processes of the VA makes all the difference in how quickly your claim will be reviewed – and approved.

CHAPTER FOUR

GIFTING CAN BE HAZARDOUS TO YOUR HEALTH - and WEALTH

We've all heard that a little knowledge can be dangerous, and when people finally realize that they could lose their home and life savings to a nursing home, they panic... and start giving all of their money away to their kids. They deed their homes to their children and put their children's names on their bank accounts because they think that will protect them. Nothing could be further from the truth! Asset protection is confusing, and rather than addressing (and paying) for proper estate planning, many seniors are tempted to just give their stuff away. This is a huge mistake. In fact, it is the most common - and most dangerous - financial planning error made by seniors and retirees today.

Don't Let Your Kid's Problems Bump Into Your Money

We have a golden rule about gifting in our office: Don't ever put in your son's name what you wouldn't put in your daughter-in-law's name, and don't ever give to your daughter what you wouldn't give to your son-in-law. And we know that all of you readers just love your daughters-in-law, right? Maybe you have a wonderful daughter-in-law or son-in-law. But statistics tell us that 1 in 2 marriages end in divorce. And unfortunately, divorce changes people. It can turn the sweetest woman into a raging lunatic, and her divorce attorney will have no qualms about coming after your bank accounts because your son's name is on them. That's right, his divorce can bump into your money. And when his wife's attorney files the divorce complaint, he will request all assets in your son's name. Your son will be required by law to list your bank accounts. **BAM!** Just like that, your CDs, money market and checking accounts are all exposed as potential marital assets that might be snatched up by your greedy daughter-in-law and her nasty divorce lawyer!

What if your children aren't married or are already divorced? Well, they drive, don't they? And what if your daughter has a car accident, is proven to be at fault and is sued for more than her auto insurance limits? The injured person's attorney will be coming after any bank accounts in your daughter's name – including yours. Now perhaps you will succeed in convincing a judge that the account belongs to you, not your daughter, and that you simply added her name to the account to avoid probate or to permit her to sign checks. But why put yourself in that position? Do you really want to jeopardize your money that way? If you want to avoid probate, you can put a transfer on death designation on your accounts, or transfer them to a trust. If you want your daughter to sign your checks, you can grant her limited signing power on your account, or better yet, sign a proper power of attorney appointing her to sign checks and other documents for you.

Before you add your child's name to your bank accounts, ask yourself this question: Do you know how much credit card debt your child has? Are you really familiar with your child's credit scores? Oh - how times have changed! Instead of sending out mass mailers offering 0% interest to hundreds of thousands of prospective customers, credit card companies are aggressively pursuing repayment from customers who are in default on their credit cards. If your son is one of those customers that hasn't paid his bills, his credit card company may sue him and obtain a judgment – then try to collect from any assets in his name. Your child can't say, "Oh, no, I'm sorry,

Visa, that money is really my mom's money." They don't care. Your child has legal ownership of the account and owes a legitimate debt. And once again, your money is in jeopardy of being attacked by a lawsuit.

If you aren't sure that your children are current on their mortgage payments, or have adequate auto or homeowner's insurance coverage, you better think twice before adding their names to your bank accounts or those accounts may become targets for their judgment creditors. Worse yet, if your daughter and her husband haven't paid their taxes, the IRS may freeze all accounts in their names (including yours). And you can kiss your money goodbye!

Are you starting to see why it's a really bad idea to put your children's names on your bank accounts? Despite what your bank teller or hair dresser may be telling you, adding your children's names to your bank accounts or real estate does NOT protect those assets from a nursing home crisis. If your name remains on the account, the state Medicaid office will follow the "source of funds" rule. If you are the only one who put money into the account, the state will consider the entire account as a resource available for payment to the nursing home. The only potentially protected dollars are those that you can prove your child deposited into the account. If you don't get any asset protection, why do it at all? To avoid probate? There is a much safer way to avoid probate – it's called a revocable living trust. We'll discuss that trust in detail in our Chapter on solutions to these common problems.

There's No Place Like Home – Which is Why You Better Hang On to It!

Like your bank accounts, adding your child's name to your real estate deed does nothing to protect the asset from a nursing home. If your name is still on the deed, the state will view it as your property and it may not be completely insulated from the "spend down" or from estate recovery. Despite this fact, seniors love to put their children's names on their deeds. Even worse, many deed their real estate outright to their children and remove themselves completely. There is no other way to put this – **DON'T DO IT!!!** It is a terrible idea to deed your home to your children for numerous reasons.

First, as we discussed above, your children's problems can easily become your problems. If your son gets divorced, your daughter-in-law may wind up owning your house...and kick you out! If your daughter is sued or files bankruptcy, your home may be attacked as an asset in a lawsuit or bankruptcy court. This could jeopardize your continued ability to have a roof over your head. Let's consider an even worse scenario:

Francis is a widow whose husband Jack passed away last year after a long battle with Parkinson's Disease. Francis has already lost a great deal of money paying for her husband's nursing home care. Determined to protect her home from her own possible health care crisis in the future, Francis deeds her home to Robert, her only child. Robert has been married for six years and has no children. His wife Jeanne has never been close to Francis, and Francis has always disapproved of her daughter-in-law. She is lazy, never cooks or cleans, and spends too much of her son's hard-earned money at the mall. But Robert loves her and Francis knows he will never leave her.

One day Robert is commuting home from the office and is in a horrible car crash…and is killed. Of course, Francis is overcome with grief. She doesn't know how she will live without him. Soon, she will have another problem… <u>where</u> she will live. Because upon Robert's passing, his Last Will and Testament states that all of his possessions are to be devised to his wife Jeanne. He and his wife had their Wills drafted years ago and Robert never realized he should change it to address his mother's home. And because of the horrible relationship between Francis and Jeanne, guess what happens? Jeanne tells Francis to get out! That's right, Jeanne now owns the home where Francis has lived for the past fifty years. And Jeanne has the legal right to evict Francis and move herself in – or sell the home and snatch up all of the sales proceeds. Surely this *is not what Francis hoped to accomplish when she deeded her home to her son. Unfortunately, that is the result, and there is absolutely nothing Francis can do about it now. What a tragic outcome for Francis.*

Remember, if the unthinkable happens, and your child dies before you, your home, your bank accounts, and everything else that you have transferred outright to him may become a part of his estate. If he has a Will, it probably states that upon his death all of his possessions go to his wife. If he doesn't have a Will, the intestacy laws in most states will probably direct everything to his wife as well, or to his wife and children. Either way, if your child owns your house when he dies, you could be moving out real soon. You may not end up in a nursing home, but you may end up on the street! Are you starting to realize why this is such a bad idea?

Need more convincing? How about an increase in your taxes? Many seniors have finally obtained a homestead exemption on their real estate taxes, and are paying less property tax than they have in the past. But if they deed their house to their children, they will lose their homestead exemption because the house is no longer in their name. Worse yet, because the children are now the actual owners but the parents continue to reside in the home, the real estate will be taxed as non-owner occupied (rental) property, which is taxed at a higher rate. Guess what else increases when a home becomes non-owner occupied? Your homeowner's insurance! That's right - when you deed your home to your children, you increase your own taxes and homeowner's insurance premiums! Actions you take to try to preserve your assets can actually deplete them more quickly.

In addition to increasing your property taxes, you make an even costlier tax mistake when you deed your home to your children. Because when you give your house to your kids, you also give them your cost basis. "Basis" is the term used by accountants to describe the amount you paid for your house (or stock and other investments). Let's see how this works.

Joe and Marge Johnson purchased their lovely ranch home in 1957 for the whopping price of $35,000. That means that their cost basis in the property is $35,000. (If they made some improvements over the years and have kept good financial records of those improvements, they could add those costs to their basis as well). In 2010, Joe and Marge deed their home to their two kids, Joey and Cindy, to avoid probate (which it will) and protect the home from the nursing home (which it will after five years). Joe and Marge continue to live in the home for many years, and fortunately their children have not divorced, filed bankruptcy, been sued, nor died. After Joe and Marge pass away, their children list the house for sale. The real estate market has been good in the area, and the home is *now worth $235,000. The children are happy that the house sells for such a large amount...until their accountant informs them that they owe capital gains tax on $200,000. That's right, by deeding their home (and their cost basis) of $35,000 to Joey and Cindy, Joe and Marge created a voluntary capital gains tax for their children! In our office we call that a **thirty thousand dollar** mistake!*

Too bad for Joey and Cindy. If only their parents had done proper estate planning they could have avoided this voluntary money snatcher. Surely Joe and Marge didn't want their kids to pay **$30,000** in taxes when they got the family home. If Joe and Marge had left the home to their children through their Wills, Joey and Cindy wouldn't have had to pay any capital gains tax when they sold the home. That is because they would have received a step-up in basis[26], meaning their basis would not have been what their parents paid for the home. Rather, their cost basis would "step up" to the current market value of the property. So if they sold the house for its current value of $235,000, they would have experienced zero capital gain – and paid zero capital gains tax. This is clearly a better result, but would not have avoided probate. A properly drafted revocable living trust, however, would have avoided probate *and* eliminated the capital gains tax.

What if Joe and Marge were concerned about a future nursing home crisis? If they had been properly informed, they could have deeded their home to a special purpose asset protection real estate trust. This would have protected the home from a nursing home crisis, avoided probate, *and* eliminated the large capital gains tax to their kids. Wouldn't that have been a better result for this family?

You see, with proper planning, you can transfer wealth to your family and avoid probate costs without putting yourself and your assets at risk. You can solve your estate planning problems without creating new ones. Get help, get informed, and ensure the proper result for your family in the future without harming yourself right now.

Gifting and Medicaid –
THINK BEFORE YOU GIFT!

In Chapter Two, we discussed the Medicaid penalties that can be created by gifting. Thanks to the Deficit Reduction Act of 2005, gifting is one of the most dangerous things you can do. Because the government changed the look-back period from three years to five years, all gifts made within the previous five years must be reported on your Medicaid application. Every state has its own penalty divisor, which is an amount chosen by each state based (loosely) on the monthly cost of nursing home care in that state. The penalty is calculated using a state-specific divisor which is typically between $5,000- $6,000.

If a Medicaid applicant has transferred or gifted assets up to the amount of the penalty divisor, it will create a one-month penalty. If the penalty divisor is $5,000, then every $5,000 that was gifted creates a one-month penalty. If a father gave his son $10,000, a two-month penalty will be assessed against him.

Prior to the passing of the Deficit Reduction Act, you could give away about $5,000, and within a month that gift would be safe. Not anymore. Now, each and every gift that you make will be counted against you for the next five years, and you will be penalized for it. The government doesn't come in and assess a fine against you, or take your money - it simply refuses to pay your nursing home bill for the number of months assessed as your penalty.

Assume the penalty divisor in your state is $5,000. This means that if you gave away $5,000, that "gift" creates a one-month penalty, meaning Medicaid will refuse to pay your nursing home bill for one month. Think of the look-back period as a big black hole. Everything you owned or gave away in the last five years is in that hole, and when you file an application for Medicaid, the state will look at all gifts that you made during that previous five year period. Every $5,000 you gave away during that time period will create an additional month where Medicaid will refuse to pay your bill.

In order to fully explain how the new rules work, we will compare them to the old rules, which are the rules prior to February 8 of 2006, when the Deficit Reduction Act was actually implemented into law. Let's look at an example where grandma helped her granddaughter and got herself in a real pickle.

Grandma has very little money other than a $50,000 CD. She makes ends meet just fine on her small fixed income and has been saving that CD for a rainy day. She's so proud of her granddaughter because she's been accepted into a prestigious medical school. They have always been close, and rather than passing it on to her when she dies, she would like to help her granddaughter now. So grandma cashes out her $50,000 CD and gives it to her granddaughter for tuition, room and board.

If the penalty divisor is $5,000, that $50,000 gift made by grandma would create a 10-month penalty. Remember, every $5,000 gifted creates a one-month penalty. By dividing the amount of the gift ($50,000) by the state penalty divisor ($5,000) we arrive at the penalty (10 months). Let's examine the impact of this gift under the old, pre-DRA rules. If grandma gave the money to her granddaughter on January 1, and then at Thanksgiving time she has a stroke, and by December she leaves the hospital and has to go to a nursing home, will this gift disqualify her from Medicaid based on the penalty period? Well, under the old rules, the 10-month penalty period would have started the day she made the gift. So let's count the months: January – February – March - April – May –

June - July – August - September – October - November – December. By December, 11 months have passed. The gift created a 10-month penalty, so the $50,000 gift is safe. Granddaughter can keep the money and use it for her education - exactly what grandma wanted.

Unfortunately, grandma would have a very different result under the new rules. Thanks to the Deficit Reduction Act, for all transfers made on or after February 8, 2006 (the effective date of the DRA of 2005) the penalty created by the gift will not start until the nursing home resident applicant actually applies for the nursing home. Effectively, that means no gifts are safe unless five years pass after you make them. All gifts that fall in the black hole (the immediate five year period prior to entering the nursing home) will be brought forward to the date of application and will be treated as if the Medicaid applicant made the *gift that day*. Then the penalty period starts running – while you are in the nursing home – and you will be facing huge monthly bills until the penalty period expires.

Let's revisit grandma under these new rules. Grandma gifted $50,000 to her granddaughter in January 2010. Grandma's health is fine in 2011, 2012, 2013, and 2014. Her granddaughter has completed her coursework and is starting her residency. In November 2014, grandma has a massive stroke and needs immediate 24-hour skilled nursing home care. Granddaughter is the only living relative. She is still in school and doesn't have the means to properly take care of her grandmother in her incapacitated condition.

Granddaughter explores different nursing homes and locates one that will give grandma good care. The cost is $7,000 per month. Upon the advice of the social worker at the nursing home, granddaughter visits the local Medicaid office to apply for assistance for grandma. As she is completing the application, she reads a question asking if grandma has made any uncompensated transfers (gifts) of money or property in the last 5 years. Well granddaughter asks the Medicaid caseworker about this question. "Excuse me," she says, "my grandma didn't really give me a gift, but she did pay my tuition in medical school." Well, that is a gift in the eyes of Medicaid, and because it was made during the last five years prior to applying for assistance, it falls in the black hole and is counted against grandma. And because of the changes in the law, Medicaid treats the gift as if grandma gave it to her granddaughter *today!* As we now know, that $50,000 gift created a 10-month penalty, so Medicaid tells her they are sorry, but grandma is disqualified from Medicaid for 10 months.

The state basically says we are not going to help grandma pay her nursing home bill for 10 months because she made a transfer for less than fair market value. The state refuses to help, and the nursing facility calls granddaughter to inform her that the family must private pay. When she tells them she has no money (because she spent the $50,000 already and she doesn't have a paying job yet) and grandma has nothing of value left either, the Medicaid office won't care. They will refuse to help. Remember, Medicaid presumes grandma gave that money away so she wouldn't have to give it to the nursing home (even though she was in good health at the time and just wanted to help her granddaughter). The nursing facility cannot be expected to accept a non-paying patient for ten months. They would eventually go out of business for providing free care.

Now there is a gap in payment here. On her fixed income, how will grandma afford to pay a $7,000 per month nursing home bill? If granddaughter can't come up with the money, how will grandma get the health care that she needs? Granddaughter may drop out of school and try to care for her grandmother, but she couldn't possibly provide 24 hours of skilled care by herself. As a result, grandma's health is going to suffer and she will be at serious risk of injury and neglect. Because of grandma's generosity, she has unknowingly compromised her own health care.

The point is, anytime senior citizens make gifts, they too could be unintentionally jeopardizing their future health care needs. Medicaid will even try to snatch gifts to your grandchildren or donations made to your church or favorite charity. Even innocent transfers can cause very long periods of ineligibility for Medicaid. Outright gifts of money, stocks, and bonds are obviously uncompensated transfers that will be held against you. Less obvious transfers, like putting your child's name on your deed, or loaning your daughter the down payment for her home and later forgiving the debt, will also be viewed as impermissible gifts. Some creative folks might give their son $10,000 to paint their porch. Well, that's not going to fly with Medicaid because the state can do a fair market value assessment. So if the average charge to paint your porch was a thousand dollars and you paid your grandson $10,000, Medicaid will treat that as a $1,000 compensated transfer and a $9,000 gift – and penalize you for it.

Penalties also apply if you allow someone to withdraw money from a joint bank account. Say you have your son or your daughter on your checking account and that account has a balance of $100,000. Your child quickly withdraws $50,000 because you've been diagnosed with Alzheimer's and need nursing home care. Your money is not adequately protected because the state has the right to review your check registers and bank statements for the last five years. And you can bet they will carefully scrutinize large transfers of money made within a few months of an application.

- Medicaid is Tougher Than the IRS! -

We are definitely at the point in this discussion where many folks will say "Now wait a minute…aren't we allowed to give away $10,000 a year without a penalty?" Well, folks, that is an IRS rule, and although it is now indexed up to $13,000, the rule permits you to gift $13,000 per person per year (annual exclusion) without those gifts counting towards your lifetime exclusion. Remember: That is an IRS rule, NOT a Medicaid rule. You should know by now that Medicaid doesn't permit you to give anything away, and will penalize you if you do. While one branch of the government clearly authorizes gifting, another branch punishes you for the same actions. The IRS (notoriously the biggest money-snatcher known to man) gives its blessing and Medicaid gives you a penalty. No wonder everyone is so confused! Remember, Medicaid treats all uncompensated transfers as thinly disguised attempts by seniors to avoid paying the nursing home, regardless of their health when they made them. So think before you gift! Your future health care just might depend on it.

CHAPTER FIVE

TAXES: A TWO HANDED BANDIT

One snatcher you just can't ignore is taxation.

You know the old saying "You can't avoid death and taxes". While there is definitely some truth to that statement, this Chapter is dedicated to controlling the impact of taxation. How can you decrease the financial and estate planning impact that taxes will have on you and ultimately on your family? There is a lot of "penny wisdom" floating around out there, and too many unsuspecting families who realize their missteps all too late become very "dollar foolish". Tax mistakes can be the most costly money snatching errors. Some of the worst tax losses suffered can feel like this snatcher dove in with both hands and robbed you blind.

Let's start with a basic premise here: Taxes ARE going up. It's already on the books - and heavier tax burdens are on the way. Just look at the cost of all the recent Government bailouts! As we write, the dollars spent are reaching epic proportions – so high in fact it's hard to describe, but we'll try our best for you. Probably the best authority out there today on how the Government has gone crazy is the Peter G. Peterson Foundation. In the Foundation's March 2009 "State Of The Union's Finances: A Citizen's Guide" the following statistics were revealed: *The Current Liabilities and Unfunded Promises of the US Government total $56.4 TRILLION Dollars.* Now that number is even scarier to us than the National Debt, which is only a mere $11 TRILLION. The liabilities include promised dollars for Medicare benefits in the amount of $36.3 Trillion, $6.6 Trillion for Social Security benefits and $13.5 Trillion for "other liabilities".

We are obviously a very indebted Nation. But how's our cash flow? In the last 50 years we have had a balanced budget only six times. If you exclude using Social Security funds to supplement the budget, it's been balanced only once. This debt and the future "legacy" costs associated with Medicare and Social Security are a perfect storm set up for a weak dollar. In fact, Chinese premier Wen Jiabao publicly expressed his concern regarding the creditworthiness of the US Government.[27] His concerns are legitimate because without reform, federal deficits and debt levels will rise so high relative to our country's Gross Domestic Product (GDP) that it threatens our economic strength and eventually our national security. As mandatory expenses rise, defense spending continues to be cut. Defense spending since 1968 has been cut by more than 50% as a percentage of total Federal Spending.

To make this personal, the Government's fiscal hole creates an individual financial burden of $184,000 on each person living in the US today. Limited to full-time workers, that number jumps to $435,000 per person. If you take a ride down any average neighborhood street, each household you see is fiscally responsible for $483,000. If you thought the Government wasn't going to raise your taxes, reading those statistics should have quickly cured any delusional thoughts you may have been having about future tax increases.

In fact, tax laws have already been established and tax rates are going up. The capital gains tax in 2011 will increase from 15% to 20%. Income taxes also are scheduled to increase.

In the face of expanding taxation, what can we offer as hope to you, the reader of our book? Be tax savvy with your money; not all investment and savings vehicles get taxed the same, so do your homework and choose wisely, and don't create a voluntary tax that could have been avoided.

In a nutshell here's what works:

When can you tax defer? For working folks this might mean using tax deferred plans like your 401(k) plan. If you have the option to use a Roth 401(k) plan, jump on it. Unlike the traditional 401(k), the Roth 401(k) offers no immediate deduction, but all the growth inside of the account can be distributed in retirement totally tax free. And if you don't need the money there is no Required Minimum Distribution from a Roth 401(k) or Roth IRA so you can literally build a huge tax-free inheritance for your family.

Tax Deferred Annuities. Somebody, somewhere started this whole "annuities are bad" kick and wow (!) what a disservice they have done to retirees. While we admit that most annuities offer little benefit, the right annuity structured properly can give you 100% peace of mind that neither you nor your spouse will ever run out of money. No mutual fund, stock or bond can promise that tremendous benefit. Frankly, the financial media gets a ton of money from the mutual fund industry, and they are most likely the source of the annuity bad press. Don't buy into that press. Be an informed consumer, but don't dismiss annuities as a financial planning tool. They offer many benefits unavailable through any other financial vehicle.

Nothing is better than tax free! Tax deferral is great, but somebody eventually pays the tax bill. Tax-free benefits, on the other hand, are the ultimate tax-planning nirvana. No other product can better transfer your wealth totally tax-free than life insurance. Your beneficiaries receive the death benefits of your policy with absolutely no tax. Many retirees shy away from life insurance because it makes them face mortality. While that is perfectly understandable, guess what? We are all going to die someday. You know the old saying, "only two things in life are certain...death and taxes"? When dealing with life insurance, only one of those things is certain, because when you die your family receives the life insurance benefits <u>tax-free</u>. What a wonderful way to transfer wealth to your family. The use of properly structured life insurance can dramatically enhance a retiree's estate plan and totally disinherit the IRS. Tax-free wealth transfer - it's just too good not to consider.

WARNING: The authors of Money Snatchers frequently use very specific annuities and life insurance products held in proprietary trusts created specifically to enhance the benefits of the annuity and/or life insurance product used. You, the reader, should not view our comments here as a blanket endorsement of annuity contracts nor of life insurance products. In most situations, neither option is totally effective without the careful wrapper of a protective Trust.

So, there you have it - a few suggestions on how to curb your tax liability with more tax- friendly assets. That said, a much more ferocious money snatcher lurks in the world of taxes that can easily be avoided by the informed consumer. What makes it most troubling is that this horrible money snatcher is an invited guest into the purses and wallets of retirees. This is one of the most common mistakes made by seniors and retirees, who unknowingly create voluntary taxes for their children.

"It's All About Basis Betty" – It's About BASIS!!!!

God bless Betty! Betty longed for what she called the "simple days". We knew exactly what she meant. There we were, the authors, meeting with Betty and explaining why she needs all sorts of planning… and we literally watched as her eyes glazed over and she tuned us out. Her very next words were these … "Why can't I just give the kids my house and the stocks… this is all so confusing. Why does everything today have to be so complicated?"

We felt bad for Betty. Here's what she owned:

- 38,500 shares of General Electric. Her father, a former GE engineer, was a huge believer in "his company." Betty inherited these shares from her father and when he died the shares were valued, with splits and dividends not reinvested, at $164,780. Over time, the shares increased in value to over $1,000,000, and then decreased to their current value of $677,600.

• Betty's home, that she bought thirty-eight years ago for $29,400, is worth $245,000 today.

We knew we needed to help Betty work through the math because she was thinking about just giving all of her "stuff" to her kids to protect it from long-term care costs. But it's just not that simple. We needed to show Betty why that would be a very costly error. So we asked Betty "How much tax did you pay on those GE shares you inherited from your dad?" "Well, I don't believe I paid any." "Yep, that's right Betty. You got what the IRS calls a step-up in basis."

We knew we needed to help Betty Avoid A Potential $109,263 IRS Tax Snatch!!!!

We also knew that in 2011 the snatch would be even worse – that her desire to give her "stuff" to her kids could cost them $145,684!

Let us explain the math. When Betty inherited her father's shares, she received a step up in basis to the market value at the date of his death. That means that the IRS views the GE shares as if Betty paid $164,780 for them (her cost basis). If she gifts her GE shares to her kids *before* she dies, she also gifts them her cost basis of $164,780. But they are actually worth $677,600. So when the children sell the stock, the IRS will expect her children to pay tax on a **$512,820** capital gain ($677,600 current value minus $164,780 tax cost basis). **OUCH!** The house gets the same tax treatment. If Betty gifts her $245,000 home to her children during her lifetime, she also gifts them her cost basis (what she paid for it) of $29,400. The capital gain is calculated by subtracting her cost basis (her purchase price plus any verifiable home improvements) from the current value of the home. Current market value ($245,000) minus the cost basis ($29,400) equals a **$215,600** capital gain!

The collective capital gains tax would be based on the $512,820 gain on the stock and the $215,600 gain on the home totaling $728,420. In 2010, the capital gains tax is 15%, so the tax cost would be $109,263. In 2011, the tax rate, by law, increases to 20%, so Betty's mistake becomes much more costly … at $145,684!

Now here's the killer… With proper planning, Betty's children wouldn't have to pay a single dime of tax - not even a penny! Without the proper information, Betty – and so many parents just like her – will unknowingly create a voluntary tax bill for their children simply because they choose to take the "simpler" approach to estate planning... with a very costly result. You see, it's easy to jump to "let's just put it all in the kids' names" because you seem to get some real benefits from what on the surface appears to be a rather simple solution:

A. You automatically avoid probate; and
B. In 60 months you get protection from a nursing home long-term care need.

Well, it's true. Adding your children's names to your bank accounts does avoid probate, and probate on an estate of $922,600 could easily go north of $30,000 in costs and fees. Plus, with care costs around the country ranging from $6,000 to $9,000 EACH and EVERY month, there's a great deal of motivation to move that money out of your names and away from a nursing home - if you really trust your kids.

But remember: you don't want your children's problems to become your problems. Hopefully Chapter Four has already opened your eyes to the dangers associated with this old-fashioned (and out-dated) strategy.

The good news is ... there is a better way.

Certain properly designed Trusts could allow Betty's children to retain her step-up in basis (saving Betty's family at least $109,263); remove the assets from her probate estate (saving Betty's children at least $30,000); eliminate the possibility of her children's potential divorce, lawsuits, credit card debts, bankruptcies from bumping into her money (safeguarding Betty's $922,600); and protect Betty's assets from a Medicaid spend-down scenario (possibly saving $920,600, in addition to the State's individual asset allowance which is usually $2,000).

Here is a parting shot on taxes. Betty had some significant bucks. But even if you have more modest assets, such as a house worth $180,000 with a cost-basis of $40,000, you could easily make a $21,000 tax mistake. Planning ahead to avoid these costly errors is much less expensive than trying to "rig up" a do-it-yourself plan that <u>cannot</u> be fixed once the mistakes are made.

So, be tax savvy ...defer, defer, defer and when you can go tax free. And most importantly, don't rely on outdated, simple estate planning. Doing so might just make it simpler for the IRS to snatch up your money by handing it to them on a silver platter!

CHAPTER SIX

SECRET MONEY SNATCHERS...sssshhhhh!

We need to warn you. Some money-snatchers are lurking in the shadows, waiting to pounce when you least expect it. Others are right out in the open and seem innocent enough, yet can have devastating financial consequences. Read on and learn how to spot them before they strike.

HIDDEN MEDICAL TAXES
(Beware - They're Comin' After Your House!)

Under current Medicaid laws, when a Medicaid recipient dies, the state that paid his nursing home bill must try to recover from the decedent's estate the total amount of money Medicaid paid out for his medical care. This process is called *estate recovery*. It's the Federal government's way of forcing every state to recover money previously paid out in the form of Medicaid benefits.[28]

If the spouse of the deceased Medicaid recipient is still living, no recovery is supposed to take place until the spouse dies. Likewise, if a child of the deceased recipient is under the age of 21, or is blind or disabled, estate recovery is not permitted.[29]

According to estate recovery rules, states are required to attempt to recover funds from the Medicaid recipient's probate estate (what passes through their Will after they die). The most commonly targeted asset is the real estate titled to the decedent at death. But Medicaid also gives each State the option of seeking recovery against property owned by the Medicaid recipient that is *not* a part of the recipient's probate estate. This includes jointly held bank accounts, real estate held jointly with rights of survivorship, assets held in a Revocable Living Trust, and life estate interests in real property.

Because of Medicaid's strict asset limits and spend-down requirements, most people who previously qualified for Medicaid benefits won't have many assets of significant value in their probate estate – except maybe the family home. Remember, in most states your principal residence is exempt when you apply for Medicaid, so it is not counted as a resource that would disqualify you from benefits. When you die, however, estate recovery rules turn this exempt asset into a countable resource – and give the states the green light to come after it with a vengeance. That's right – if the state paid your nursing home bill, it can snatch your house away from your heirs when you die!

While some states, like West Virginia, vehemently opposed the implementation of estate recovery, others have broadened their estate recovery rules to include personal property and non-probate assets like real estate held jointly with rights of survivorship, life estate interests and transfer on death deeds. States are aggressively pursuing the recovery of Medicaid benefits by attacking seniors' homes after they die. The states typically employ "outside counsel" (a fancy term for a hired gun attorney) to file liens against your real estate to ensure that the State recovers all of the money it paid out for your long-term care expenses. Because these lawyers are paid a percentage of all monies recovered, they have a huge incentive to collect every dime possible from your estate – and away from your family.

Although the estate recovery attorneys cannot force your surviving spouse to vacate your home after you die, if the state files a lien or Affidavit of Lien against your estate, it will create a cloud on the title to your real estate. In other words, if your spouse or children try to sell or mortgage your home after you die, they may be forced to deal with (and pay off) the State's lien before enjoying any of the proceeds for their own benefit.

So let's revisit John and Mary. Remember, John was required to spend all of his money (except $2,000) before

Medicaid would help pay his nursing home bill. Mary was forced to live on less income, because John's income went to the nursing home, and she also lost half of their assets. Three years after qualifying for Medicaid, John dies. Mary decides to sell their home and move to a smaller place near her daughter. She lists the house for sale with her friend who is a realtor. The potential buyer does a title search of the real estate records in the county courthouse, which reveals a lien (disguised as an Affidavit of Title) against Mary and John's home. Mary gets the surprise of her life! She had no idea this lien was filed against her property in the courthouse records – nobody ever bothered to tell her! And now when her house is sold, the buyer's attorney (and his mortgage lender) will require that the Medicaid lien be paid off and removed from the title before closing can occur. After all, nobody is willing to buy property without a free and clear title. Mary's buyer is no exception, and he refuses to purchase the home unless the government's lien is released. When the house is sold, part of Mary's settlement proceeds must be used to pay off the lien. This means that Mary will have much less money than she counted on, because she never counted on hidden medical taxes snatching up such a big chunk of the family home.

But wait! Estate recovery is not supposed to occur as long as the Medicaid recipient's spouse is living. This lien should never have been filed in the county records until both John and Mary died. If Mary knows this, or hires an experienced elder law attorney who does, she may be able to prevent the state from snatching all of her proceeds when her home is sold. Otherwise, the state – and the state's attorney – may be getting paid before Mary does. What if instead of trying to sell the home, Mary lives there until she dies? She may die never even knowing that the state filed a claim against her real estate. And John and Mary's children will inherit their parent's home subject to the state's lien. Because once John and Mary die, the state's attorney can come after the home with guns blazing – and at that time, the most experienced attorneys on the planet can't prevent John and Mary's children from watching their inheritance go up in smoke.

So not only is the cost of long-term care a real money snatcher, Medicaid – the system that you turn to as your last hope for help – is a real money snatcher too. It takes all of your income and at least half of your assets, and then comes back for your house when you die. Your home - which you thought was an exempt asset during your life – is really a countable asset that the Government will attack upon your death. Talk about a secret money snatcher! In our office, we call these hidden medical taxes, because if you are on Medicaid, you will be totally unaware that the government is running a tab, and they'll come collecting from your heirs after you die.

THE GRIM REAPER

You don't need to read a book to understand the devastating emotional effects of losing a loved one. But many are not prepared for the harsh financial impact they will experience if their spouse dies before they do.

In most cases, when one spouse dies the Social Security shuffle occurs. The surviving spouse is not permitted to keep both social security checks previously enjoyed by the household. Instead, she retains the higher of the two. In other words, if a husband's Social Security check is higher than his wife's, when he dies she will lose her smaller Social Security check and gain his. If you are already living on a fixed income, having your Social Security check snatched away from you could cause serious financial harm.

Many unsuspecting seniors experience a significant loss of income due to straight single life pensions. If a retiree elected to take his pension "straight" that means that it is only paid out during his lifetime. When he dies, the pension dies with him, and his wife gets nothing. In our local steel mill town, most retirees have straight single life pensions; this is quite common in mill and factory towns all over the country. Many retirees were never given another option or were never properly advised of the effects of a straight life pension. Others felt they had to choose this option because they needed the additional retirement income. They assumed they would save enough money to ensure the surviving wife would be well provided for if her husband died before her. What they didn't factor in was the possibility of a long-term illness draining their life savings.

Let's take a closer look at how one retiree's straight life pension can have devastating consequences for his spouse.

Bill is 70 years old and Ruth is 68. Of significance is the life expectancy tables set forth in the Health Care Finance Act Transmittal 64, which indicates that females have a seven year life expectancy advantage over males. None of us have a crystal ball to predict how long we will live; however, when doing estate and asset protection planning for Bill and Ruth, we must consider that it is quite possible that Ruth, who is two years younger than Bill, may outlive Bill by nine years.

Bill's monthly income is comprised of $1,200 from Social Security and an $1,800 pension. Ruth's Social Security is $600. They have about $300,000 in the bank. The Social Security shuffle happens when Bill dies, because at that point Ruth will inherit Bill's $1,200 – but lose her $600. Many folks are totally unaware that this will occur. It is especially important for elderly women who have never worked outside *of the home. If your husband passes away, you will inherit his Social Security if it's larger than yours, but you don't get to keep two. You lose your Social Security benefits. So while Ruth inherits $1,200, she loses the other $600. Her new Social Security income is $1,200.*

When Bill retired from the steel mill, he took his pension straight. This means that when Bill passes away his pension dies, too. Ruth will lose another $1,800 per month, and her total household income (currently $3,600) will drop to $1,200. What we call that in our office is "moving to a new neighborhood." Because it is unlikely that Ruth can maintain her present standard of living on 2/3 less income. How many of us could?

Now if we are meeting with Bill and Ruth for planning, this is about the point where Bill will tell us "yes I am aware of all this. That's why we saved $300,000." But do you remember John and Mary? What if Bill winds up like John, in a nursing home for over three years? He and Ruth could lose more than half of their money before Bill dies. And Ruth, who will be trying to live on 1/3 of the income she previously enjoyed, will be forced to spend her share of the money to help pay her bills...and their children will get next to nothing. And when Medicaid starts paying the nursing home bills, they'll be planning on coming after the house later - so the kids won't get that either.

This happens all too frequently to married couples who worked hard and saved their money. The husband wants to ensure that his wife will be provided for if he passes away, and the wife wants to ensure that something is left for the children. That's what Bill and Ruth wanted, too. Unfortunately, a straight life pension and an unexpected illness can snatch away those plans in a second. Proper Income and Inheritance Trust Planning (discussed in Chapter Eight) can help preserve Bill's pension for Ruth, even if disability strikes first, and ensure an inheritance for their family.

PROBATE: WHERE THERE'S A WILL... THERE'S A BILL!

Probate is a formal legal process designed to settle a deceased person's debts and transfer assets to their heirs in an orderly and supervised manner. It is often a lengthy and drawn out process that prolongs the ultimate distribution of your money and property to your family. It can delay the sale of your real estate as buyers and their mortgage lenders require clear title to the property. Because of its public nature, it can create a breeding ground for family disputes and a feeding frenzy for hungry creditors. Complex filing requirements and paperwork typically require legal expertise – which can be quite pricey. Probate costs vary from state to state –the range is generally 3% - 8% of the value of your estate. So when your children inherit your money and property through your Will, they also inherit a hefty bill to go along with it.

The probate process begins when your Executor (the person you appointed to handle your estate after you die) takes your Will to the courthouse and files it in the county of your legal residence. Once recorded, your Will becomes a matter of public record. Your Executor must do an inventory of everything you owned at your death, and determine its worth. He must then file an appraisement listing the title and value of all of your real and personal property passing through your Will, including your home, bank accounts, stocks, bonds, and vehicles – everything titled in your own name at your death. This appraisement also becomes part of the public record and can easily be viewed by anyone who is curious about your wealth and your heirs. An advertisement is published in the local newspaper to inform the public of your passing. This is essentially an invitation to your creditors to file claims against your estate to recover unpaid debts. It can also turn your surviving spouse into an easy target for predators to swindle her inheritance or steal her identity. If you owned property in another state, an ancillary administration must be filed in the other state as well. In other words, your heirs may be hiring two separate attorneys (and paying two separate bills) in order to settle your estate and actually take possession of your assets.

What so many folks don't realize is that probate is not inevitable. It can easily be avoided… but remember, don't try to fix a future problem for your heirs by creating worse problems for you and your spouse while you're living. You should already know from reading Chapter Four that adding your children's names to your bank accounts and real estate deeds exposes you to serious financial risk. Rather than choosing that outdated planning technique, use specialized Trusts instead. They will help you to eliminate probate, not your bank balance!

WALL STREET: Double Fisted Snatchers

This isn't about Bernie Maddoff. This isn't about Ponzi schemes and white collar criminals. The money snatchers revealed in this section are perfectly legal. Protecting yourself from being fee-snatched and over-taxed is really about knowledge. Knowledge is Power! So, take another sip of that coffee (or better yet, a highly caffeinated Mountain Dew) and take this information in………… then go check your statements.

Mutual Funds: One of the favored investments of Wall Street is the mutual fund. It is marketed as a vehicle that provides diversification with the oversight of an experienced money manager. Sound good? Well, in theory it makes sense, but not all mutual funds are built the same way.

Mutual funds offer different share classes. An A-share mutual fund has an upfront load. A load is the commission you pay to buy the fund. A-share mutual fund loads can range from 3% on bond funds to 5.25% on stock funds and specialty funds. So, immediately the mind says "A-shares are bad because I don't want to pay that load". That's one of the scariest things about money snatchers: what seems like the right answer is usually wrong.

All mutual funds (including so called no-loads) have an expense ratio. An expense ratio is what the money management firm charges the client for the management of the fund. These fees can be all over the board, ranging from very low to painfully high charges. In the red hot days of the Internet bubble, technology "no load" funds charged investors ongoing annual fees of 3% of their account value. A load like that could certainly snatch a lot of money out of your account. Although A-Shares may come with an upfront commission, they typically offer the lowest on-going expense ratio, often making the A-share purchase option your best buy.

Two share classes that make little sense are B-shares and C-Shares. B-shares look like *no-load funds*, but there's a catch. The "B" actually stands for a back-out fee. So, if you sell early - you pay. Worse, you pay more as you go because B-Share funds typically have higher expense ratios (aka: management fees). The additional fees help the mutual fund companies recapture the commission they paid to the selling broker. B-Shares are no free lunch. B-Shares are, in our opinion, just bad for consumers.

C-Shares are not much better because they add the commission onto the expense ratio. If a money management firm charged a 1% management fee and your advisor sold you a C-share fund, then an additional 1% commission is added to the 1% management fee for a total annual fee of 2% - OUCH! So, C-shares for very short-term investing might make sense. But, in reality, you shouldn't be investing for the short term, so C-shares are a money snatcher for sure ... it's like building an annuity for your advisor! Investing should really be about **your** retirement, NOT theirs.

Fee-based money management may be better, in certain circumstances. However, the costs associated with your investments are not eliminated by a fee-based advisor. This type of advisor is going to tack his fee onto your initial investment costs. Fee-based management fees can range from fractional percentages to 2% or more. Again, the fees you pay can overwhelm your portfolio's performance.

Hidden Mutual Fund Money Snatcher: The Ever Present, Seldom Discussed Money Snatcher: Turnover Ratio

Mutual funds buy and sell stocks at the direction of the money manager who manages the fund. So, if a mutual fund has a turnover ratio of 100% that means that in one year the whole portfolio has been sold and new positions bought. Now those "trades" aren't free. There are transactional expenses in the form of commissions which are paid to the brokerage house to facilitate the trades. In most cases, the mutual fund company _owns_ the brokerage outlet through which it buys and sells the stocks and bonds. The reason turnover ratio is a hidden, sneaky money snatcher is because these companies don't make it easy to see how much has actually been paid for the trades. Is that a conflict? Definitely. The question stands: How much does turnover cost? This is difficult to answer. We estimate (meaning no study has validated this figure; it's just our belief) that a 100% turnover equates to approximately a 1% additional "cost burden" to the fund assets. OUCH! Are you realizing that, once again, you've been *money-snatched?*

How To Avoid Turbo-Charged Taxation On Your IRA!!!!

Obviously, turbo-charging your IRA tax burden is NOT a good thing. Taxation, without turbo-charging, is already a big enough money-snatcher; you certainly don't want to add fuel to that blazing hot fire. IRA planning in America is kind of funny. Almost every advisor on every street corner is talking about distribution planning and what to do when you turn 70 ½ - seniors seem to like to talk about it…. A hot button, if you will.

But here's the thing: IRAs aren't really assets at all. By law, they are a tax-deferred savings vehicle to supplement your future retirement. The good old IRS keeps its hands off until you reach age 70 ½, but then you have to start paying your partner (Uncle Sam). That's really deferred compensation. You took money out of your paycheck, grew it tax-deferred so that you could have money later on in retirement. Conceptually it makes a great deal of sense.

Now a few of you with large IRA accounts are probably a little angry at us right now for claiming that your biggest account isn't really an asset at all. Just give us a moment to prove this to you. Simply call your bank and ask how much collateral value they assign to an IRA. That call will validate our point - because the response will be <u>zero</u>. What's the reason for this? The money in the account is not really all yours. Some of that money is in that account to pay the IRS. Because the account does not clearly define how much of that money is for tax dollars versus how much cash is yours, the account is truly valueless collateral to your bank until you start taking withdrawals.

As if that isn't bad enough, Wall Street and a few big insurance companies have found a way to make this IRA problem a whole lot worse.... And what we are about to reveal is virtually unknown. Treasury Regulation 1.401 (a)(9)-6 redefines the Required Minimum Distribution calculation: If the death benefit or the income benefit of your annuity, owned inside of an IRA, exceeds the underlying cash value of the annuity by more than 20% it becomes a *safe harbor provision.* This means the Required Minimum Distribution (RMD) is calculated from the actuarial value of the death benefit or income benefit and not from the actual value of the annuity.

Let us explain the ramifications here. Let's say you own a variable annuity and the cash value of the mutual funds inside the annuity is $96,842, but the death benefit is $176,458 at the end of the year. Now, let's say you just turned 70 ½ so you are required to take a distribution. The amount of the RMD is based on the IRS uniform lifetime table. According to the table, at age 70 ½ the divisor is 27.4. Therefore, to calculate RMD you divide the account value by 27.4. In this case the RMD would be $96,842 divided by 27.4, requiring a **$3,534.38** distribution – right? **WRONG!** This IRS rule requires you to use the death benefit of $176,458 as the account value when calculating your RMD. The RMD equation now becomes: $176,458 divided by 27.4 = **$6,513.07.** While the distribution is *calculated* on the death benefit, the money is *actually coming from* the mutual funds currently worth $96,842. Translated into a percentage, we divide the $6,513.07 distribution by the $96,842 actual account value to equal 6.725%. How long will your account last with those huge percentage distributions? ...Not as long as you thought!

When the account value zeros out, guess what? The death benefit disappears! So, this nasty money-snatcher gets you two ways: First, you'll be paying all of those extra fees along the way and, second, you are likely to lose the income benefit or death benefit if you have longevity (exactly the opposite result that most folks buying these benefits are actually expecting). Protect yourself from this money snatcher by realizing that if you own a variable annuity inside of your IRA, with these added "sizzle" benefits, like death benefits and income benefits, the IRS expects you to pay tax on the entire interest of that IRA... and you may very well lose the extra benefits you've paid for.

How Do You Protect Yourself From Becoming A Fee-Snatched Victim of Wall Street?

Always make sure you are getting value for your money. There should be a fair amount of contact and communication between you and your management firm or advisor. And the contact we are referring to should be *to* you, not *from* you. You are **paying** for their services – they aren't FREE. It makes sense that your advisor should keep you apprised of the status of your account and in tune with whether your current account performance remains consistent with your overall goals. There's nothing worse than getting "sold" by a financial salesperson dressed up like a real advisor. By definition, an advisor should be advising you! Demand nothing less from yours.

WARNING: This should not be interpreted as encouragement for you to do it yourself. Let's be blunt – you may be the greatest dentist, doctor, lawyer or bricklayer your town has ever seen. But these skills in no way transfer into investment super powers, and you will not become the next Warren Buffet just by reading a few paragraphs in a book. There is nothing worse than snatching yourself of your own money through delusional ideas picked up from a book or an on-line course. That said, smart money management does require that you play an active role in your own investments. Just don't let your pride get in the way of your common sense. Get help from experienced professionals. Ultimately, it is your responsibility to clearly articulate your goals and question all investments, insurance and savings products selected by your advisor, to ensure that they are in line with your stated retirement and estate planning goals.

BUILDING A SOLID LEGAL FOUNDATION

One of the most important things you can do to develop a plan that will withstand a future disability is to build a solid legal foundation. While many see the wisdom in getting their legal "ducks in a row," most don't realize that not all legal documents are the same. In fact, common errors in your basic legal documents can actually trap your money and wipe out your life savings if disability strikes.

When doing estate planning, the most common course of action is to visit the family attorney and obtain a Will. Everyone knows that someday they are going to die, and are generally concerned with who gets their assets when they are gone. Too often, that document sums up most estate plans, because people continue asking that old estate planning question…"What happens to my stuff when I die?" That kind of obsolete planning really misses the mark today. AARP, MetLife and GE Financial all predict that at least 1 in 2 of us will need some type of long-term care in the future.[30] Now that doesn't mean that 50% of us are headed for the nursing home, but at least half of us will require some kind of long-term health care – so we better have a plan to pay for it without going broke.

Are you prepared for a future of expensive home health, assisted living, or nursing home bills? If not, perhaps you need to start asking the new question in estate planning… "What happens to my stuff if I become disabled before I die and need long-term care?" You may have given some thought to temporary illness or a trip out of the country, and asked your lawyer to draw up a Power of Attorney – maybe you even printed one off of the Internet. If so, are you certain that document is powerful enough to protect your money and your house from being lost to nursing home bills?

You will be shocked to learn how traditional estate planning documents can create insurmountable problems if you or your spouse get sick – problems that can never be fixed unless caught in time. Be sure that your legal documents don't destroy your ability to protect your lifesavings if disability strikes. Read on to learn how to identify the most common errors contained in almost all traditional estate planning documents. We'll tell you how to spot them right away, and help you to avoid being the architect of your own future financial disaster.

What's With All These "Bad" Documents?

You are probably asking yourself why so many of these "bad" documents exist. Surely there can't be that many lawyers out there who don't know how to draft Wills, Trusts and other basic estate planning documents. Well the problem isn't that these lawyers are incompetent. But they are practicing traditional estate planning, and that is really death planning. When a client visits an estate planning attorney, their biggest concern is that their money and their home go to whom they want without dispute or delay. You will see in the next few paragraphs how traditional "death planning" can actually have the opposite result.

The I Love You Will – Love It Or Leave It?

The most basic of all legal estate planning documents is a Last Will and Testament, and many single folks without children don't even bother to get one. As for most married couples, you can bet they have traditional "I love you" or "Sweetheart" Wills. The husband's Will states that when he dies, all of his just debts and expenses are to be paid, and the remainder of his estate goes to his beloved wife. If his wife dies first, then his estate goes to the children. The wife's Will is a mirror image of her husband's, devising all of her assets first to her husband, and then to the children. Each spouse is named to serve as each other's Executor, and the oldest child is typically named as the alternate. These Wills often comprise a married couple's entire estate plan.

So what is wrong with that? Well, first of all, if your goal is to leave assets to your loved ones without dispute or delay, you will probably not accomplish that with an "I love you" Will - or with any Will, for that matter. A Will forces your estate into probate, which can cause great delays and disputes, and can be very expensive. But there's a bigger concern with the old "I love you" estate plan. Today, we know that 1 in 2 Americans face the need for some type of long-term care assistance – and some of those people will end up in a nursing home. The average cost of a nursing home today is about $6,000 per month, and as you have now learned, Medicaid won't help you pay that bill until you have spent virtually all of your assets down to $2,000. That's right – your entire life savings could be wiped out before the government helps you with your biggest health care expenses.

Let's revisit John and Mary. They have been married for 48 years. The family lawyer drafted their "I love you" Wills 30 years ago to ensure that their children (and future grandchildren) were taken care of when they died. Many years later, John suffers a debilitating stroke and is forced to go to the nursing home. Remember what happens to their money? Mary is overwhelmed with worry about her husband's health care, and with how she is going to pay the $6,000 nursing home bill and still maintain her home. She is "spending down" a large portion of their assets on the nursing home and is trying to live on a reduced income and half of their assets. The stress of her husband's poor health and the financial burden prove to be too much for Mary, the supposed "healthy" community spouse, and guess what happens? She dies first. What happens to John and Mary's money? Well, Mary's traditional "I love you" Will leaves everything she owns to her beloved husband, who is in the nursing home. It all becomes the sole property of John, who *is racking up that $6,000 per month* healthcare expense. He will be forced into a "spend down" that ends in most states when there is only $2,000 left. The question now is this: Have John and Mary's estate planning goals been met? Of course not, because now their children and grandchildren will get nothing.

If only John and Mary had asked the new question in estate planning, and obtained an "I love you dearly ¬BUT" estate plan! They could have utilized special Trusts that direct assets *away* from a disabled spouse if the other passes away first. They could have preserved their money for Mary and passed on assets to their children, instead of losing everything to the nursing home. When doing planning, be sure you are asking the right question. Don't just plan for death. Plan for disability, too. Otherwise, the nursing home might end up being your biggest heir.

Is There A Bear Trap In Your Trust?

Maybe you have discovered a viable alternative to those traditional "I love you" Wills - and transferred your home and your bank accounts into a Revocable Living Trust. A Trust is a document containing  specific instructions concerning how your money and property should be managed when you are alive and ultimately distributed when you die. Trusts can either be revocable (you can change, amend or eliminate it at any time) or irrevocable (more permanent and unable to be changed) or sometimes a unique hybrid of the two.

Conceptually, a Revocable Living Trust (RLT) makes perfect sense. Traditional estate planning attorneys will explain that this Trust helps you to avoid probate - and that is true. The cost and delay associated with probate make an RLT a very attractive tool. Even if a married couple owns their accounts jointly (which avoids probate between the spouses) this trust avoids probate for their children too. A Revocable Living Trust is typically structured so the Grantor (who created the trust), the trustee (who manages the trust) and the beneficiary (who benefits from the trust through income or access to principal) are all the same person or persons.

So, consider another couple – Fred & Wilma – who have transferred their bank accounts and home into a Revocable Living Trust so that when they die, their daughter Pebbles will inherit everything without the delay and expense of probate. Before their deaths, Fred and Wilma have full access to the money in the Trust. They can modify the terms of the Trust, spend all the money in the Trust, change the beneficiaries or even get rid of the Trust altogether (revoke it). They have complete control. It's truly a revocable Trust.

Because Fred and Wilma were such good savers, and Fred had a strong pension from the rock quarry, they have accumulated $200,000 in their Flintstone Family Revocable Trust when Fred passes away. After Fred's death, Wilma continues to have complete control over everything in the Trust. Like before, the problem comes when disability strikes. Years later, Wilma is diagnosed with Alzheimer's disease. She is no longer able to manage her own affairs, and despite her daughter's best efforts to keep her at home, Wilma now requires 24-hour skilled nursing home care for her own safety. Pebbles takes charge of the assets in the Trust because her parents had designated her as the successor Trustee.

What else has changed about the Trust? Although the Trust was revocable by Fred and Wilma, the original trustees, it is **NOT** revocable by the successor trustee. Pebbles is required to follow the terms set forth in the Trust, and will breach her fiduciary duty if she doesn't. So, is there a problem? If the Flintstone Family Trust looks like most Revocable Living Trusts out there, you can bet your bottom dollar there is. Traditional estate planning attorneys almost always include health, education, maintenance and support language (often referred to as HEMS provisions) in the successor trustee section of the Trust. The Trust actually dictates that the Successor Trustee (Pebbles) must use the Trust assets for the health, maintenance and support of the Grantor (Wilma). What is the true impact of this language? Well let's consider Wilma, who is mentally incapacitated but physically in good health. She may spend years in a nursing home at a monthly cost of more than $6,000. Her daughter will be forced to spend almost ALL of the $300,000 to pay nursing home and health care bills, and will get no help from Medicaid until that money is gone. Why? Because the Trust requires that the money be used for Wilma's health, maintenance and support...in other words, the nursing home!

HEMS provisions appear in almost every RLT ever drafted - we see them all the time. If they are in your Trust, it may be impossible for your family to protect any of your assets if you end up in a nursing home. Just a few sentences in a document that you *PAID FOR* can literally trap your life savings and force your children to give all of your hard-earned money to the nursing home. Without them, Pebbles could have preserved a significant amount of that $200,000 – which her parents worked a lifetime to save – and kept it in the family where it belongs.

A cautionary word about Revocable Living Trusts... they are NOT asset protection Trusts and do NOT protect your "stuff" from the nursing home. How can you tell if your Trust is protected from long-term care costs? If you have direct access to the Trust assets - can reach into the accounts and withdraw money, or sell your real estate and keep the sales proceeds - without any assistance from anyone else- then those assets are NOT protected. If you can get to the money, you will be required to get to the money...and spend it on your care...before getting any help from the government.

Do You Have A Powerless Power Of Attorney?

A power of attorney may be the single most important document in your estate planning toolbox – yet most people don't ever obtain them. If you get sick and can't communicate or make decisions for yourself, the agent you appoint in your health care power of attorney will have the right to talk to your doctors,  authorize medical treatment, and have full access to your medical records. A financial or general durable power of attorney gives your agent the right to access your bank accounts and sell real estate. This appointment is especially important if you become disabled because without it, it will be very difficult for anyone to protect your assets from being wiped out by long-term care costs.

If you have a financial power of attorney, how can you be sure that it is really powerful? We've all heard that the road to ruin is paved with the best intentions. Many well-meaning estate planning attorneys add gift-giving limitations to the document, such as: "My agent is hereby prohibited from making gifts to himself or herself." So if you become incapacitated and your wife is your agent, she will not be allowed to use any of that money for herself. Many powers of attorney will only permit your agent to make gifts "up to the annual exclusion". That refers to an IRS rule that allows you to gift $13,000 per year per person without it being counted towards your life-time gift tax exclusion. Most people know they can give away $13,000 a year (it used to be $10,000) without a penalty – what they don't know is that referencing that rule in their power of attorney can trap all of their money to pay for their future long-term care.

Let's think about John and Mary again. Suppose John has a $275,000 IRA (individual retirement account). Because IRAs cannot be jointly owned, the IRA is in John's name only. John has designated Mary as his primary beneficiary so when he dies, Mary gets the money. But that kind of planning doesn't address the new question in estate planning, does it? Because what happens to John's IRA now that he is disabled and entering the nursing home? As a beneficiary, Mary has no right to John's IRA until he dies. If prior to becoming mentally incapacitated John did not sign a power of attorney appointing Mary as his agent, she can not access that IRA and try to protect it. She will be forced to seek guardianship and conservatorship rights over her disabled husband. She has to hire a lawyer, go to court, and ask that John be declared incompetent, which can be a horrible and expensive process. Then, a judge gets to decide what Mary can do with John's IRA (that she was supposed to inherit) and could order her to use the money to pay for John's health care instead of preserving it for her and her husband.

Good thing John had the foresight to get that Power of Attorney and appointed Mary to handle his finances. But is it truly powerful? Well, if John's lawyer included those gift-giving limitations in his document, Mary may be able to protect only $13,000 of his IRA - and the rest could be lost to the nursing home! This is an example where language designed to protect you (from a tax standpoint) can create much more harm than good...and by the time you realize this costly mistake is in your documents, it will be too late to fix it.

So look carefully at your legal documents. Look for limitations on gifting in your Powers of Attorney, and look for Bear Trap language in your Revocable Trust. Seek advice from an experienced elder law attorney who can help you fix these problems before it's too late - and build a solid legal foundation that you can truly count on if disability strikes.

CHAPTER EIGHT

IT'S NOT ALL BAD NEWS

THERE ARE THINGS YOU CAN DO...

Here Are Some Powerful Solutions....

GET OUT YOUR TOOLS AND BUILD A FORTRESS AROUND YOUR MONEY

Your first line of defense from all of the money-snatchers we've discussed is to build a solid legal foundation. The sooner you start laying the groundwork, the better. You accomplish this by having a powerful power of attorney and carefully designed Trusts that specify how your money and property should be handled in the face of disability and the crushing financial burden of long-term care costs. If you have large IRAs or other qualified accounts, be sure your Power of Attorney doesn't contain gift-giving limitations that prevent your spouse from accessing and protecting your assets. If you have a Revocable Living Trust, look carefully for those HEMS provisions – and get them removed! And remember, be aware - or BEWARE - that not all legal documents are constructed the same. Finding the right legal assistance from an experienced elder law attorney is the key to avoiding legal mistakes in your documents that could trap your money and make the nursing home your biggest heir.

Your Last Will and Testament and wealth transfer documents should be constructed to "disinherit" a disabled loved one who may be receiving public benefits. If receiving an inheritance will ultimately cost your loved one valuable assistance in the form of government benefits, then it is better to direct your assets to a protected account that can be used for your loved one's needs without disqualifying them from benefits. Otherwise, your money will be used in place of those benefits until it runs out, which is probably not what you intended when you had your Will drafted. If your goal is to preserve assets for you and your spouse, and transfer wealth to your children when you die, this is best accomplished through the use of special Trusts that will safeguard your money if disability strikes. Because when dealing with long-term health care, when you're out of money, you're out of options. And being broke – and at the mercy of the government- is a place you never want to be.

The right Trust planning can pave the way to a solid estate plan that truly protects your wealth and your health! Your own set of instructions, chosen in advance, can direct your money *to* your family and *away* from creditors (nursing homes, your son's unpaid credit card companies, your daughter's bankruptcy) predators (divorce and your bad daughter-in-law, high-priced probate lawyers) and a government gone wild (taxes, estate recovery).

PLANNING FROM BOTH SIDES OF THE COIN

After constructing a solid legal foundation, it is important to target the financial outcome you desire. This is best accomplished by integrating carefully drafted trusts with very specific financial and insurance products. This is not commonplace in the retirement planning community for two very silly reasons. First: Most lawyers think they know everything and don't need any help. Second: Most financial advisors think they know everything and resent the lawyers who often oppose what they perceive to be risky financial strategies (and counsel their clients to reject them). The financial advisor is portrayed as a product pusher with no real value to add to the estate planning equation. In reality, the proper coordination and cooperation between these two specialties can greatly contribute to a sound estate planning process. But this big personality clash, and a continued lack of understanding of how each can benefit the other, perpetuates this outdated, one-sided planning that leaves your assets at risk and the door open for the invasion of the money snatchers to barge in and swipe precious dollars right out of your bank accounts. (See, we told you it was silly but that is the truth!) When doing your estate planning, be sure you have a multidisciplinary team of professionals working for you. That way, you'll have all the bases covered (financial and legal) to help make your plan a home run.

IF GIFT YOU MUST... GIFT TO A TRUST

Transferring money within the family, especially to family members you trust, is a great strategy to protect assets from long-term care risk. But the money-snatching risks associated with gifting are so high, we need to summarize them again... and then craft a better plan.

BIG Gifting Risk Number One: Your *children's* problems can bump into *your* money. One in two marriages end in divorce; drivers have auto accidents;

your children or their spouses (remember, you always wanted your daughter to marry a doctor!) may have huge professional liabilities; the younger generation has much more debt than you do, and they love to use those credit cards. Your children may strap themselves with high mortgage payments, open-ended lines of credit and car loans, leaving them overextended and ripe for lawsuits from money-snatching bill collectors. <u>Don't Forget:</u> If you put your children's names on your bank accounts and real estate deeds, you are paving the way for their creditors to get reimbursed – with your money and property!

<u>BIG Gifting Risk Number Two:</u> Thinking that Big Risk Number One isn't a concern for you because your children and their spouses are perfect! If that is true, you are very fortunate. But no matter how wonderful your children may be, they still drive, work and get married, all of which can expose your assets to money-snatchers beyond their control. And remember, outright gifts to your perfect children may cause them to pay large capital gains taxes, receiving a less than perfect inheritance.

Making gifts to revocable Trusts with your children as named beneficiaries is a smarter way to keep wealth in the family by avoiding probate and preventing a disabled spouse from inheriting assets that will be lost to the nursing home. Using irrevocable and "hybrid" Trusts can protect your assets from future long-term care costs. We utilize a proprietary technique we call the Protected Gift Account. This strategy permits you to make completed gifts to family members without exposing your money to their creditors or creating large capital gains. Gifted funds are held in a "safe harbor" account designed to work with a specially drafted protective Trust. Taxes are deferred, probate is avoided, assets are protected...a smart way to make gifts that keep on giving!

IF YOUR HOME IS YOUR CASTLE, YOU BETTER BUILD A MOAT!

For many folks, the family home is often their largest asset. When you consider the added sentimental value, it's easy to see why this is one of the largest areas of "do-it-yourself" planning. Unfortunately, it is also the area where the some of the biggest mistakes are made. While it makes good sense to protect your home from all of those money-snatchers out there, we hope that Chapter Four has opened your eyes to the dangers of deeding your home directly to your kids. If you want to avoid probate, transferring your home to a properly drafted Revocable Living Trust is a smarter way to accomplish that goal. Likewise, the proper asset protection Trust can protect your home from nursing home bills and estate recovery. But Remember: not all Trusts are the same. The wrong language in your Trust can turn into a powerful Bear Trap; if disability strikes, that trap will clamp down so hard you will never get your money out, and the nursing home will become your biggest heir.

Life estate deeds, once a very popular estate planning tool for probate avoidance and asset protection, should be used with caution. A life estate interest is the right to occupy, possess and use property during your lifetime. This right exists as long as the owner of the life estate interest is alive; when they die, the life estate interest dies with them. If you deed your home to your children and reserve a life estate interest for yourself, you will retain the right to live in the home. That right cannot be compromised by your children's debts, divorce, or lawsuits. As the owner of a life estate, you will have a present right of ownership (life estate interest) and your children will have a future right of ownership (remainder interest).

Unfortunately, life estate deeds are overused and misunderstood, and the protections they afford are often exaggerated. Big problems can arise if your house is sold while you are still alive. If you are a healthy senior who intends to use your sales proceeds to purchase new property, travel the world, or make investments, you may not realize that your children are entitled to a portion of the proceeds (which increases as you age). They are entitled to keep part of the money, leaving you with less money than you may have been expecting. The older you get, the less your life estate interest is worth, and the less you will be entitled to keep if the house is sold. In order to transfer ownership to the new buyer, your children (and in many states, their spouses) must sign the Deed. If they refuse to sign, they can interfere with your ability to sell your own home!

If you are a disabled senior now living in a nursing home, and your children sell your house, they may not realize that you are entitled to a portion of the sales proceeds. The percentage of your ownership interest is legally set by state statute (but if you're on Medicaid, federal life estate valuations may be used). When the house is sold, your portion of the proceeds will be at risk of being lost to the nursing home (and can cause you to lose your Medicaid benefits until the money is spent down). And if you have a lengthy nursing home stay and your home isn't sold until after you die, the new estate recovery rules will require the state to come and snatch your life estate proceeds...even though you are no longer alive! It's crazy but it's true. The states are permitted to value your life estate *right before you die* and file a lien against your home for that amount.

In order to fully protect your home, don't rely on outdated planning methods. Properly drafted asset protection trusts can avoid probate and protect your home from future long-term costs while still keeping a roof over your head.

BRINGING DEAD EQUITY BACK TO LIFE

Millions of seniors are struggling to make ends meet without realizing they are surrounded by available money. It's all around them, in the walls, floors and ceilings of their home. They just need to pull it out. Unfortunately, less than 20% of retirees ever use their homes to help fund their retirement, and of those, only 5% ever do so with a reverse mortgage.[31] This is a severely underutilized and totally misunderstood financial tool that if used properly, can be a real powerhouse estate planning strategy. Contrary to popular belief, a reverse mortgage does *not* require you to sell your home to the government. Instead, you are loaned money based on the value of your home, and you are never required to make a monthly payment. The accrued interest on the loan is rolled into your total mortgage balance. The house remains in your name until it is sold. When you pass away, your heirs can choose to pay back the loan and keep the house, or walk away and let the bank sell it. Either way, your family will never be personally responsible for that debt. When your home is ultimately sold (by you while you are living or by your heirs after you die) none of you will ever be required to pay back more than the market value of the home at the time of the sale, regardless of the loan balance.

Pulling the equity out of your home to pay off all of your debt or go on a mad spending spree are probably not the most advisable uses of a reverse mortgage. And most retirees, who take pride in the fact that their home is paid off, would never even consider using their home as collateral. But the fact is, if you are pinching pennies and still drowning in bills, this strategy could be the proverbial life raft that gets you safely to shore.

For those who are living comfortably, reverse mortgages present unique planning opportunities to protect your future healthcare (and keep you out of the nursing home) and guarantee a tax-free inheritance for your family. This is the essence of the "Spend It Twice" strategies proposed by Matt in his book of the same name. A reverse mortgage is utilized and funds are paid out in one lump sum payment (an allowable distribution option). A portion of the mortgage proceeds are then used to purchase a life insurance policy with a special long-term care rider. Enough life insurance will be purchased to replace the value of your home that would have been inherited by your children mortgage- free. If you become disabled, and begin failing routine activities of daily living, you can turn on the switch and the rider starts paying out a set monthly amount for home health care, assisted living, or even skilled nursing care. Unlike long-term care insurance, however, if you never need the long-term care money, the policy remains intact until your death, at which time it is distributed to your heirs – tax-free and without probate.

A WORD ABOUT LONG-TERM CARE INSURANCE

Another gigantic warning! Long term care insurance doesn't usually cut it. It is experience rated, like your auto and homeowners' insurance. If the experience of the insurer is unfavorable and they are losing money, they can increase your premiums. This is typically done when you are older, on a fixed income and approaching the age where long term care is a real risk factor. Suddenly, you may be faced with the decision to either increase your premium (which swallows up more of your income), or reduce your coverage, at a time when the costs of long-term care are going to be much higher than when you originally bought the policy. Coverage is generally inadequate, and if you never use it, you lose it. In theory, long-term care insurance sounds great. In reality, it may wind up snatching more money than it protects. It may become too expensive to maintain, may provide inadequate coverage, and may give you a false sense of security that prevents you from planning appropriately. The smarter solution: Avoid the marketing hype. Steer clear of long-term care insurance and opt for life insurance with fixed premiums and long-term care riders. That way, you'll know just what to expect in terms of costs and benefits.

INCOME & INHERITANCE TRUST PLANNING

You've read about the dreaded "spend down" and how skilled nursing home costs can be financially devastating to a surviving spouse. It is very sad to see the aftermath of financial ruin that long-term care costs can unleash on a family. Hundreds of thousands of dollars spent. Then pensions and Social Security checks die right along with our loved one, leaving the surviving spouse in a financial crisis. Add in the final blow, courtesy of your State and Federal Government, when those hidden medical taxes (estate recovery liens) come and snatch your home from your children. It's easy to understand why retirees and seniors today just want to stick their heads in the sand and do nothing. Confusion and fear often lead to inaction. That, unfortunately, is the path to certain failure, with so many snatchers lurking in the wings ....
That's why it's an invasion. Not one snatcher, but many snatchers, all coming from a different perspective or from

a different governmental agency, can wreak havoc on a surviving spouse.

What can we do to protect a spouse's income and then ultimately pass wealth on to their family? We utilize a strategy we call Income and Inheritance Trust Planning. Just like the Protected Gift Account, success comes from a carefully crafted trust document paired with a specific insurance-based product. (Again, legal and financial concepts combined to produce the best results). Here, the solution is reverse engineered. Consider a husband who is age 70, and his wife of 48 years is a healthy vigorous 68 year old woman. Statistically we know that from birth, she has a seven year life expectancy advantage and can reasonably live nine years longer than her husband. The good news is, if he is alive and in fairly good health right now, we have the benefit of time and the power of compounding interest in our favor. Planning opportunities exist – even at age 70 – to protect a surviving spouse from the inevitable income loss created by her husband's passing.

Step one is doing some simple math. We discount back to present value dollars how much income we need to replace when the husband dies. Let's say his wife's income will drop $1,500 after his death. He is currently 70 years old so his life expectancy is about 15 years. The question is: "How much do we have to put aside today so that in 15 years his wife is <u>guaranteed</u>, from a highly rated insurance company, to get $1,500 a month for her life?" In essence, the planning replaces her income she is sure to lose when her husband dies. Then, because we don't want that "pension value" to die with her, the unused value remaining is transferred – without probate - to their children. The solution is actually income *then* inheritance planning.

Financial advisors love to "round up". We totally disagree with that practice. If it takes exactly $82,437 to fix the income problem in the future then that is the amount to fund into the strategy. You should never position more money than you need to use to solve your financial planning problems. Before you embark on any estate planning financial strategies, you should develop the attitude going in that you are going to solve your retirement planning problems with the least amount of money possible – whatever that number is… and not a penny more!

At first glance, this appears to be a purely financial solution. But remember, money-snatchers come from all angles. Although the right insurance product can solve the problem of future income loss for your spouse when you die, you still must address what happens to your money if you become disabled before you die. Again, this is rarely analyzed because of the ongoing friction between legal and financial professionals. (Remember, Lawyers vs. Financial Advisors). By working with qualified attorneys, specific points of the insurance product are matched to specially designed Trusts, allowing for future income, as defined by the insurance product, to be available to your spouse post your death. BUT, don't allow them to use all of your money in this planning strategy! Because if *all* of the money is available to your spouse when you die, and your spouse ends up in the nursing home, then your plan is seriously flawed! Unless the plan properly defines that *income* and *NOT principal* is available, your planning may lead you straight into the "spend down"… and your children can kiss that inheritance goodbye!

Be sure you are working with a qualified lawyer who knows how to tailor your beneficiary designations to fit your overall financial plan. With a customized asset protection trust, your beneficiaries can be divided as: Income beneficiary, principal beneficiary and final beneficiary (at death). This way, your money can be legally directed and protected. Remember: **Don't be a victim of the word processor.** Not every Trust is the same. Income & Inheritance Trust Planning creates a targeted solution specifically designed to replace lost income for your spouse, and protect wealth transfer to your kids. Done correctly, this is a powerful strategy.

Heck, It Ain't Even Easy To Die These Days!

If a pre-paid funeral is not already in place when an ailing senior applies for Medicaid, the emotional impact of later trying to take advantage of this exemption cannot be ignored. When a loved one enters a nursing home, it is an extremely difficult time for the entire family. Family members are usually fraught with guilt over placing their loved one in a nursing home. They are often afraid that their spouse or parent may be ignored or unnecessarily medicated in a strange environment out of their control. But some families may hold onto another emotion: Hope. Hope that their husband will get better and come home, or hope that their mother will progress enough to move to a less restrictive, assisted living facility. Nothing will destroy your hope of recovery faster than heading to the funeral home to plan your loved one's funeral. And for those who have accepted that their loved one will never come home, meeting with the undertaker and picking out a casket may be too overwhelming during what is already an unbearable emotional time.

Again, the importance of early planning cannot be emphasized enough. Making your funeral arrangements in advance, when you are healthy and able to participate, can spare your family a great deal of unnecessary grief in the future. Pre-need planning can also save you money, not only because earlier purchased funeral contracts are sold at a discounted price, but because it helps prevent unnecessary up sales by overzealous funeral directors looking to cash in on your family's emotions.

Be Warned: Pre-need funeral contracts don't come without their share of risks. Because despite the best intentions of most funeral home directors, each year we hear of unscrupulous funeral home operators and outrageous actions connected to the funeral home industry. In 2008, for example, Robert Nelms, the owner and president of a company that owns and operates funeral homes and cemetery property, was discovered to be conducting a trust fund scheme that defrauded residents in Osceola, Indiana of $27 million – money that was ultimately transferred to Mr. Helms and his wife. In the same year, the Ziomek Funeral Home in Livonia, Michigan closed without warning, leaving an estimated 20-100 people with no funeral contracts and no refund of their money. The funeral home had been in business in the community for 16 years. While some have recovered their money, many others lost thousands of dollars and have no funeral plan in place. Seriously, how could someone do this?[32]

Even in the absence of fraud or intentional wrong-doing by the funeral home, your pre-paid funeral contract could be in jeopardy, particularly if it was purchased before 2002. In Bessemer, Alabama, for example, pre-planners lost thousands of dollars when Bessemer Brown Service Funeral Home filed for Chapter 11 bankruptcy.

The bankrupt funeral home found a buyer who refused to honor the pre-paid funeral contracts already in place.[33] Since 2002, the law has required funeral operators to place pre-paid funeral payments into individual trust funds which cannot be touched. This should help protect later purchased pre-need contracts from the devastating effects of a bankrupt funeral home. Again, this is a perfect example of why you need knowledgeable legal counsel, because these pre-need arrangements are contracts and are legally binding.

An alternative to pre-paid funerals is the purchase of a Final Expense Trust. This is essentially a fully pre-paid single premium life insurance contract that is specifically designated for your final (funeral and burial) expenses. There is no requirement that you choose a particular funeral home and your family is spared the unsettling task of picking out your casket and planning your funeral while you are still living. Medicaid treats Final Expense Trusts as non-countable resources as soon as they are purchased, and in most states these Trusts are considered exempt assets up to $12,500 (you must confirm this with a qualified specialist in your State). Final Expense Trusts are backed by highly rated insurance companies and insure payment of your funeral expenses when you need them. The attraction is that you are in control of your money. The scandals discussed above were created by the relinquishing of control of the funds. The Final

Expense Trust is an account established by you, which is much more advantageous than an arrangement where an account is established by a third party vendor (funeral home) ultimately for your benefit, in the future, when you die.

Not only do Final Expense Trusts protect you from the difficult task of planning a loved one's funeral, they alleviate the potential risk of funeral home fraud or collapse in connection with your pre-need funeral contract.

So while pre-planning for funerals is an advisable asset protection strategy, proceed with caution. Investigate the funeral home thoroughly before writing them a check, and consider the use of a Final Expense Trust to insulate your money from the future financial instability of the funeral home and the unethical practices of the greedy money-snatchers who could be in charge of them.

CHAPTER NINE

HOW TO AVOID
A MONEY SNATCHER
INVASION

A 7 Step Anti-Money Snatchers Game Plan

STEP 1: DON'T GO IT ALONE! The rules of the game are ever changing. You need trusted guides who focus on solving these special types of financial problems. These trusted guides won't be found in the form of your favorite bank teller, nor at the local coffee shop or beauty shop. The greatest protection available will be with specialized teams of professionals who have both a qualified elder law attorney and a financial planner who specializes in asset protection. A comprehensive list of firms that meet this criteria are listed at: www.moneysnatchersbook.com

STEP 2: IF IT SOUNDS TOO GOOD TO BE TRUE, IT PROBABLY IS! It's a common and scary trend today to hear seniors who have made poor decisions based on "buying" into "great opportunities". For instance, if a financial salesperson tells you about a 9% CD (when you know darn well the bank down the road is paying 1.25% on CDs) guess what? That's a red flag – a giant waving red flag! When you hear something that sounds that good and you want to believe it's true, ask this simple question: So, what strings are attached? If they say there are no strings attached, then you need to turn and run. There are many great financial products out there with attractive features, but even the best opportunities come with rules. And these rules are the strings attached. You need to know what they are and decide if they are acceptable to you and are in line with your planning goals. Always use and trust your own good judgment and common sense

STEP 3: BEWARE OF FREE. There's NO free lunch. Marketers use bait and switch techniques. Here are a few to watch out for. First, let's dissect the free lunch and dinner seminar offer. Obviously, when you get an invitation saying, "hey, I'll buy you dinner and don't worry because nothing is ever sold at these seminars" your good old common sense should kick in and say hmm... this person is going to try to do something to get my money. RED FLAG. Now, we are certainly not saying don't go to seminars and learn. We do monthly seminars but the newspaper insert invites people to come and learn - not to come have a free steak dinner.

A few more FREE offers to be careful of. There are organizations who say they help veteran's get benefits for FREE. In reality, the VA *forbids* anyone from charging a veteran to file a VA application. So they aren't allowed to charge you anything. These offers are typically made by salesmen trying to sell you financial products. You can only get help with VA matters from a Veteran Service Organization (like the VFW), an accredited agent or a certified lawyer. Again, these FREE offers can end up costing you money, so watch out for them.

Lastly, watch out for insurance products with a bonus payment. A bonus technically is an immediate "dump in" of cash from the insurance company. It's certainly an inducement to buy a product and is a perfectly legal and suitable offer. However, be sure to always ask: "What strings are attached here?" With bonus products you have longer periods of back out fees. If short term funds are used to purchase the bonus product this is a huge money snatcher because the penalties are always bigger than the bonus. For longer term funds these bonus products offer a kick start that can really add value. Again, don't lose your common sense: if someone is telling you there's something for nothing – turn around and run!

STEP 4 – WATCH OUT FOR LEGAL ADVICE FROM NON-LAWYERS. We know the value of integrating trust documentation and specific financial products. However, be very cautious when the purchase of a financial product also entitles you to free legal documents to support the plan. This is where you can be penny wise and fortune foolish. Our business model is designed for collaboration among like-minded professionals focused on meeting the goals of the client. No one professional can wear all of these hats and be good at all of these jobs. We are huge fans of multi-disciplinary lawyers who understand how to carefully integrate financial solutions with specialized trusts to meet their client's goals. We have the privilege to work, as service providers, with many of America's best law firms. As accomplished as they are, even the best of the best (like Rick Law in Chicago) divide their firm's legal services and financial activities… because no one professional can do both jobs well. A key defense from being money-snatched is to realize that legal documents cost money, and a packaged offer with legal documentation included based on the purchase of a financial product is another GIANT red flag.

STEP 5 – BEWARE OF ON-LINE "RESOURCES". Information on-line should be viewed with a very skeptical eye. Today it is not uncommon for retirees and their children to get on-line to do "research". The critical question should be "are you getting information from a credible source?" This can be very difficult to decipher on-line. An additional problem is information overload. If you research the keywords "revocable trust" on Google today, you will find about 962,000 articles, websites and "resources" to review:

Google

| revocable trust | Search |

Advanced search
About 962,000 results (0.21 seconds)

The problem is, before you finished your "review" of these 962,000 "resources" you'd be dead and your family would be burdened by the cost and time delay of probate. Obviously, this would defeat your original planning goals. Now, you must do your due diligence and research but be sure your researching the right thing – getting the right help. Money-snatcher repellant tip number five: focus your research efforts on finding the right planning team to assist you. Remember Step 1 (Don't go it alone).

STEP 6 – DEMAND PROOF! There is nothing worse than getting sold a bad idea. Slick talk can be very persuasive, but in the end it may prove financially disastrous. When seeking professional advice, we recommend that you ask the following questions to ensure that you are being advised by an accomplished and experienced professional. Here's a list of good questions to ask:

a.)   **Have you ever been published in an industry periodical?** Industry magazines look for real experts to feature in their magazines so they can offer their readers credible and accurate information. To ensure that you are working with professionals who don't just talk a good game, but really know their stuff, ask if they have been featured in any magazines whose goals are aligned with your goals.

b.)   **Are you an author on this subject?** Professionals who choose to write have a passion for what they do. They've taken time to explain their beliefs and spell out their planning methods. It's not easy to write a book, so they are dedicated to their profession and proud of what they do. Plus, you can read their book and then check that the advice that they are giving you is in line with their published message.

c.)   **Do you invest in your professional knowledge?** This question is a great way to gauge the prospective advisor's commitment to staying current on new laws, tax code changes and cutting edge ideas to help preserve and grow your wealth. The same is true for the lawyers. If you have a large IRA, you might be swayed to work with an advisor knowing he has trained with Ed Slott, a leading expert CPA in the area of IRA planning. (Likewise, an advisor or multi-disciplinary lawyer who invests nearly $24,000 a year to belong to Matt's Platinum Elite coaching group is certainly educated on the latest and most effective long-term care planning strategies available to preserve and protect their client's life savings.)

d.) **Who refers business to you?** It's common to ask for references but we believe that can be a loaded question. It wouldn't be too hard for most advisors and lawyers to find three or four people to give them a good reference and say nice things about them. Our question is much different. Health care facilities refer to us because they know we help their patients pay for care and help their families. That certainly means more than handing someone a list of three or four former clients who are willing to offer praise for our services. The reason is simple: for the professional referral source, it's about getting the job done for the client. They have zero incentive to give false praise. This is a much more credible assessment of just how good an advisor or lawyer is at their craft. Again, truly effective planning advice comes from a well-organized, multi-disciplinary team of professionals (which is logical, since no one person can be good at all things.) Be sure to check them out – and be sure their references are coming from a credible source.

STEP 7 – BE SMART AND TRUST YOUR FEELINGS.
We'd love to tell you that our experience has taught us that as human beings, we make decisions based entirely on logic. But we can't. People are not wired that way. We recently had clients trying to choose between three local chiropractors in his town. It was easy to dismiss the one who wore really tacky old Hawaiian shirts with mustard stains. The choice between the other two came down to who had more literature available and how nice it looked. In essence, they both selected the same chiropractor because he had written a book and they were attracted to the book cover. We've all been taught to never judge a book by its cover – right? But that is exactly what they did. And when they went to their chiropractor's office, his polished image proved to be legit: He had awards and certificates of achievement hanging on the walls, the most up-to-date literature and state-of-the-art equipment. He

was just perfect for them. They both felt better, the service was great and although he was more expensive than the other two, our clients finished their treatment convinced that they both got great value.

The take away here this - it's ok to be attracted to professionals with well-designed materials. That shows pride. Oftentimes, the ones who appear to be the best really are! Then, when you meet face to face, gauge your emotions. If you feel comfort and a sense of greater security, then trust that feeling. Bring all the decision-makers in your family to meet the advisory team. If you all feel that the advice given was in line with their published message, and you all have more peace of mind at the conclusion of the meeting, then you've found yourself a good advisory team. When researching advisory teams, a great place to start is at www.moneysnatchersbook.com

Congratulations! You have finished the book and joined the ranks of the "informed." You should now know how to spot those nasty money-snatchers, and should be better armed to defend yourself and your family from an invasion. Now it's time to build your action plan. Like most plans, the first step is always the most critical. So roll up your sleeves, do your research, and find the team that is just right for you. Remember, early planning is smart planning. In a world full of creditors, predators and a Government that has truly gone wild, the time to take action is NOW! Stop sitting on the sidelines. Assemble your team and develop a game plan that will effectively protect your health, your wealth and your family; one that ensures you are never out of money or out of options. Then start implementing those winning strategies so you truly can live your live and forget your age.

ENDNOTES

1   LONG TERM CARE: Our Next National Crisis? A Think Tank Sponsored by the National Endowment for Financial Education, Scottsdale, Arizona - May 6-8, 2000.

2   PBS healthcare crisis: long term care. http://www. pbs.org/healthcarecrisis/longterm.html.

3   Containing US health care costs: what bullet to bite? – Cost Containment Issues, Methods and Experiences. Health Care Financing Review, Annual 1991 by Stephen F. Jencks, George J. Schreiber.

4   Fewer seniors live in nursing homes, USA TODAY, 9/27/2007, Haya El Nasser.

5   Centers for Medicare and Medicaid Services, Office of the Actuary, National Health Statistics Group, http://www.cms.hhs.gov/ NationalHealthExpendData/ (see Historical, NHE summary including share of GDP, CY 1960-2005,

file nhegdp05.zip; and Historical, Projected, NHE Historical and projections, 1965-2015, file nhe65-15.zip); cited in http://www.kff.org/insurance/snapshot/chcm030807oth.cfm.

6   http://www.newyorklife.com/nyl/v/index.jsp?vgn extoid=652d1219a49d2210a2b3019d22102430 1cacRCR

7   Lyndon B. Johnson is credited with ultimately passing the Medicare bill into law in 1965. In fact, Medicare was the brainchild of John F. Kennedy, and was the focal point of his campaign. President Kennedy began the fight for Medicare in 1961, yet after an 18 month battle was unable to drum up the necessary support in the Senate, where his Medicare bill was defeated 52-48, due to vehement opposition by the AMA. *Health Care Reform: Revising the Medicare Story, POLICY AND MEDICINE, Dec. 1, 2008*

8   Nursing Homes: Cost and Coverage, AARP.org; 2007.

9   Medicaid: The Issue, http://www.naela.org/broc_Medicaid.aspx, NAELA 2008.

10   http://www.cms.gov/MedicaidEligibility/02_
AreYouEligible_.asp#TopOfPage

11   2010 figures are subject to change as they are
affected by inflation.

12   http://www.cms.gov/MedicaidEligibility/
downloads/1998-2010SSIFBR122909.pdf. 2010
figures subject to increase).

13   *Id.*

14   Id. 2010 figures subject to increase.

15   P.L. 109-171 Sec. 6011, 6014 (DRA 2005).

16   P.L. 109-171, sec. 6012.

17   38 USC §5901-5904.

18   www.vba.va.gov/bln/21/Rates/pen01.htm;   www.
vba.va.gov/bln/21/Rates/pen02.htm

19   38 USC §1501 *et seq.*

20   www.vba.va.gov/bln/21/pension/vetpen.htm#2

21   www.vba.va.gov/bln/21/Rates/pen02.htm

22   http://www.vba.va.gov/bln/21/pension/vetpen.
      htm#2.

23   38 USC 1522(a).

24   38 USC §1503(a); 38 USC §1503(a)(8).

25   ABC News, Debbie Beckert, consultant, Assignment
      7, March 3, 2008.

26   There is no step-up in basis scheduled for the year
      2010 as of July 2010.

27   http://www.forbes.com/2009/03/13/treasuries-
      wen-jiabao-markets-economy-china.html.

28   Congress included a provision in the Omnibus
      Budget Reconciliation Act (OBRA) of 1993(P.L.
      103-66) that required States to implement a
      Medicaid estate recovery program.

29   http://aspe.hhs.gov/dalt.cp/reports/estaterec.htm.

30   http://www.genworth.com/content/products/
      long_term_care/what_is_long_term.html

http://assets.aarp.org/rgcenter/il/d19105_2008_ats.pdf

http://www.metlife.com/individual/life-advice/personal-insurance/long-term-care-insurance/index.html

31   *Spend It Twice, A Retiree's Guide to Free Money,* Matt Zagula Word Association Publishers 2009.

32   http://www.otrib.com/plan/2009/01/05/worst-funeral-home-scams-of-2008,   Emily   S. Gearson, 2008.

33   http://blog.al.com/businessnews/2010/04/bankruptcy_casts_cloud_over_bu.html.